IMAGE

Historic SUMMERSIDE

1900–1970

FRED HORNE

NIMBUS PUBLISHING LTD

THE CITY OF SUMMERSIDE / WYATT HERITAGE PROPERTIES

Nimbus Publishing Limited
PO Box 9166
Halifax, NS B3K 5M8
(902) 455-4286

Printed and bound in Canada
Design: Joan Sinclair

National Library of Canada Cataloguing in Publication Data

Horne, Fred, 1951-
Historic Summerside / Fred Horne.

Co-published by the City of Summerside and Wyatt Heritage Properties.
Includes bibliographical references.

ISBN 1-55109-385-5

1. Summerside (P.E.I.)—History. I. Summerside (P.E.I.) II. Wyatt Heritage Properties III. Title.

FC2649.S85H67 2002 971.7'1 C2002-901665-7
F1049.5.H67 2002

Canada

The Canada Council for the Arts | Le Conseil des Arts du Canada

We acknowledge the financial support of the Government of Canada through the Book Publishing Industry Development Program (BPIDP) and the Canada Council for our publishing activities.

This book is dedicated to the people who, either by design or by accident, saved old images of family, friends, communities and businesses.

It is especially dedicated to the founders and photographic professionals of Read Studio and Sears Photography of Summerside, whose policy of retaining images has resulted in a precious photo archive of Summerside and Prince Edward Island. Summerside is much the richer for the work of: Lorne Read, Delia Read, Don Sears, and Hazel Sears.

Acknowledgements

The author gratefully acknowledges the following for their support and assistance: Allan Rankin and Faye Pound, as the editorial committee and long-time supporters of this project; Sandra McIntyre and Dorothy Blythe at Nimbus Publishing; Joan Sinclair; Jennifer Wilson and Brian Hawrylak with the City of Summerside's Canada Millennium Program Project, which funded the author's participation as researcher-writer; Dutch Thompson and the participants in the Elders' Circle project, who provided an instant source of information; Donna Sears, Daphne Sears, Hazel Sears, and the staff at Sears Photography Studio; the Summerside and Area Historical Society, whose president, George Dalton, has been especially supportive; Keith Tanton at the PEI Sports Hall of Fame; The International Fox Museum and Hall of Fame; the staff at Rotary Regional Library in Summerside; the staff at the Public Archives of PEI; the staff of Special Collections at Robertson Library at the University of Prince Edward Island; the staff of Confederation Centre Library in Charlottetown; my wife, Mary Burke, for her reviews and suggestions; Allan Savidant, Susan Rodgers, Jean MacKay, and student assistant Justin MacArthur of Wyatt Heritage Properties for suggestions, support, and assistance; the thirty-plus private collectors who shared their family albums with me and whose names are included in the "Image Sources" section; and finally, a thank you to the many who shared information and images that await future publication.

Table of Contents

Legacy of the Photographers and the Photograph Collectors

THE CENTRAL PLAYER in this illustrated history of Summerside is the Read Studio, which later became Sears Photography. In operation for over ninety years in Summerside, the studio has truly been a safe harbour for the town's visual past.

Lorne H. Read was born in 1888 into a long-established and wealthy seafaring family of Summerside. He was the son of Captain Whitmore and Elvira (Davidson) Read and grandson of Ephraim and Rosara (Chappell) Read of Read's Corner. Lorne Read was close to his cousin, Captain John Read, an accomplished captain of the high seas who travelled to Canada's far north, among other places, and was the first to captain the new car ferry, the *Prince Edward Island*, on the Borden to Cape Tormentine service. Lorne took up an interest in photography at a young age—in his early teens he was out on the ice floes of the Northumberland Strait taking photos of the ice boats crossing between Cape Traverse, Prince Edward Island and Cape Tormentine, New Brunswick. This act alone produced some of the most memorable images in Prince Edward Island's photographic history.

A young Lorne Read adjusting his camera, perhaps at a favourite fishing spot on the Dunk or Wilmot river.

In 1908, Read founded the Read Studio in Summerside. A very smart man, Read liked to figure out new ways of doing things. His skills as an inventor served him well in creating "a contraption of some sort" to keep children still during portrait shoots. He also designed and built his own re-touching desk. Very early in his career, he became interested in direct colour photography, and in 1908 he produced a colour print and a colour transparency using an old process called the potato starch grain process. While the process worked, it was not very practical and only one picture was ever developed with it.

Perhaps the most exciting of Read's inventions was what could be called a "synchronized flash powder gun," which synchronized the firing of flash powder to the opening and closing of the camera shutter. According to Don Sears, Read's successor, "photographers used to set the camera on a tripod, set the shutter for a time exposure, open the shutter, ignite and fire the flash powder, then close the shutter." Unfortunately for Read, there appears to have been little interest in his invention at the time.

In 1916 Lorne Read married Delia Jane Brown, daughter of H.W. Brown of Pugwash, Nova Scotia. Delia became a partner in the photography business and was said to be particularly good with the children. Read was a romantic, interested in sea stories and adventure. He was an avid canoeist and outdoors person.

The Read Studio interior, c.1908. The north-facing skylight windows in the studio provided natural, seasonal light.

Delia shared his passion for canoeing and fishing, and was one of the first women to fly-fish on Prince Edward Island. Their favourite fishing spot was the Dunk River, which drains into Bedeque Bay. Hazel Sears remembers Delia telling her that sometimes the pair would leave the studio to go fishing on Friday afternoon and return directly from the fishing camp to the studio on Monday morning.

The couple lived in a house built by Lorne Read at 222 Church Street, across from the Baptist Church. They had no children. Delia was a great reader, congenial, opinionated, and a person with no use for gossip. Some of her contemporaries disliked her assertiveness, although she did develop a friendship with the prolific diarist Wanda Wyatt, who in her early nineties made note of Delia's passing in 1987.

Recognized as a great portrait photographer, Read went to school in Summerside and attended the College of Photography in Effingham, Illinois, earning a degree as a photographic craftsman and later as an honorary master of photography. It is believed that only ten such degrees were held in North America at the time. Among his peers, Lorne Read was well known as an advocate, joining former mentor Edgar P. Smith of Pridham Photography in Amherst, Nova Scotia to establish the Maritime Professional Photographers Association during the 1930s.

Don Sears was born in Amherst, Nova Scotia in 1924, and started practising photography at age thirteen. After graduating from high school in 1940, he apprenticed at Pridham Photography in Amherst. In 1944 Sears went oversees with the

Delia and Lorne Read in a canoe on the Dunk River, c.1922.

photo section of the Royal Canadian Air Force. He spent twenty months overseas, twelve of them on the continent following the Allied forces through France, Belgium, Holland, and Germany. He worked with reconnaissance, dealing with images taken by on-board cameras as aircraft returned from various sorties.

Sears knew a number of Maritime photographers, so after the war he toured the Maritime provinces visiting them. He heard and was soon able to confirm that Lorne Read was thinking of retiring; he entered into partnership with Read and took over the Read Studio in 1946.

In 1952 Don Sears married Hazel Barrett of North St. Eleanors. Like Delia Read before her, Hazel Sears was a full partner in the business. Hazel hand coloured photographs, becoming an accomplished colourist recognized for her work by the

Maritime Professional Photographers Association. Although direct colour came in during the 1950s, the demand for hand colouring was high because the early direct colour images tended to fade. The studio was renowned for its "island scenes," all hand coloured until the late 1960s. Hazel also ran the store. The studio was especially busy on Wednesday afternoons when the business section of town closed and weddings were common.

Lorne Read and Don Sears confer in the studio, c.1950.

In the fifties and sixties, neither Don Sears, the portrait and wedding specialist, nor George Wotton, the press specialist, had a complete set of photo equipment, so they worked co-operatively in Summerside. Following in the footsteps of Lorne Read, Sears was honoured by being named a master of photography.

The Sears family maintained a lifelong friendship with the Reads. Only in the early 1970s, when Sears moved from the original Read Studio location at the foot of Summer Street, did he change the name of the studio to Sears Photography. The old studio building was demolished to make way for the new Bank of Nova Scotia. The present home of Sears Photography is a circa-1860 building on the corner of Spring and Water streets. Don Sears died in 1992, and the studio passed to his daughter Daphne.

The work of other professional photographers from the Summerside area, such as Bowness, Clark, and Heckbert, appears in these chapters, intermingled with snapshots taken by ordinary people for whom the camera became more accessible in the first few decades of the twentieth century.

Introduction

IN THE 1830s, the three-mile-wide point on Prince Edward Island that would later be known as "Summerside" was farmland, marsh, and remnant forest. Prior to the British Empire takeover in 1758, Mi'kmaq, French, and Acadians attracted by the resource-rich Bedeque and Malpeque bays occupied the area. Around 1785, United Empire Loyalist Daniel Green settled in the area; his descendants owned one thousand acres fronting Bedeque Bay, so until the 1850s the area was known as "Green's Shore." One hundred years before the arrival of British Loyalists, most of the Bedeque-Malpeque isthmus was largely wilderness. Fourteen thousand years before that, when the Wisconsin glacier finally retreated from Eastern Canada, a once-ancient seabed became a lowland. But by 1900, the community of Green's Shore was transformed from the "tranquility of a mere rural landing place" to a "busy hive of commerce."

A new name crept into the lexicon during the 1840s when Joseph Green, son of Daniel Green, built a stagecoach inn and named it Summerside House. It seems that during construction one March day, a Major Thomas Compton, who lived at St. Eleanors on the wind swept Malpeque Bay, paid a visit to Green. On Prince Edward Island, tucked into the southern Gulf of St. Lawrence, the March winds can be more biting and raw than any other. Despite the fact that the isthmus between Malpeque and Bedeque is only a couple of miles wide, the gentle rise of the hill between them, coupled with the vegetation cover, creates a microclimate not lost on the northern visitor travelling by horse or on foot. Compton encountered Green busily cutting stove wood, probably in the shelter of his homestead. When Compton paused, he must have felt the March sun wrap his body in a blanket of warmth, for tradition has it that he turned to Green and said: "Why, you certainly live on the summer side of the island." Intrigued, Green hung a sign with the words "Summerside House" over the front door.

Usage grew and when postal service came to the area in 1852, postmaster Patrick Power adopted the name "Summerside" to distinguish the settlement from the many others around Bedeque

Bay. The Town of Summerside was incorporated with full municipal status in 1877.

Queen's Wharf, built by the government not long after Queen Victoria's ascension to the British throne in 1837, was as pivotal to the development of the village as were Joseph Green and Major Compton in naming it. Summerside House was not far from the newly constructed Queen's Wharf, primary contact point with the outside world. Just up from Queen's Wharf the main commercial corner of the town was formed where Queen Street met "Broadway," which later became Water Street but was also sometimes referred to as Front Street. From Queen's Wharf, Central Street provided the most direct access to the north side of the island, while the road at St. Eleanors did not meet the western extension of Water Street until later.

While early merchants such as James Gourlie contributed to the town's formation in the 1840s and 50s, the most extensive growth occurred in the 1860s and 70s. Compare the image at top right with the bird's-eye view from 1878 below it, and it is easy to see that a sort of boom town had developed, extending north and east.

"Summerside PEI," watercolour by Robert Harris. From the 1860s, the area west along Water Street was known as the "old village."

RIGHT: **Hydrographic survey of Bedeque Bay, 1841, by Admiral Bayfield. It shows Green's Wharf at Green's Shore as well as some early lanes and property lines.**

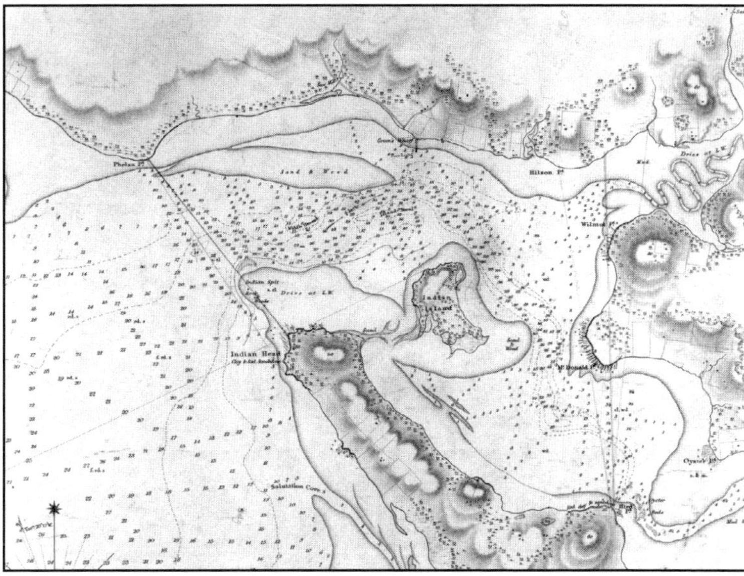

BELOW: **1878 bird's-eye view by Albert Ruger. From left to right are the Queens, Holman, and Railway wharves.**

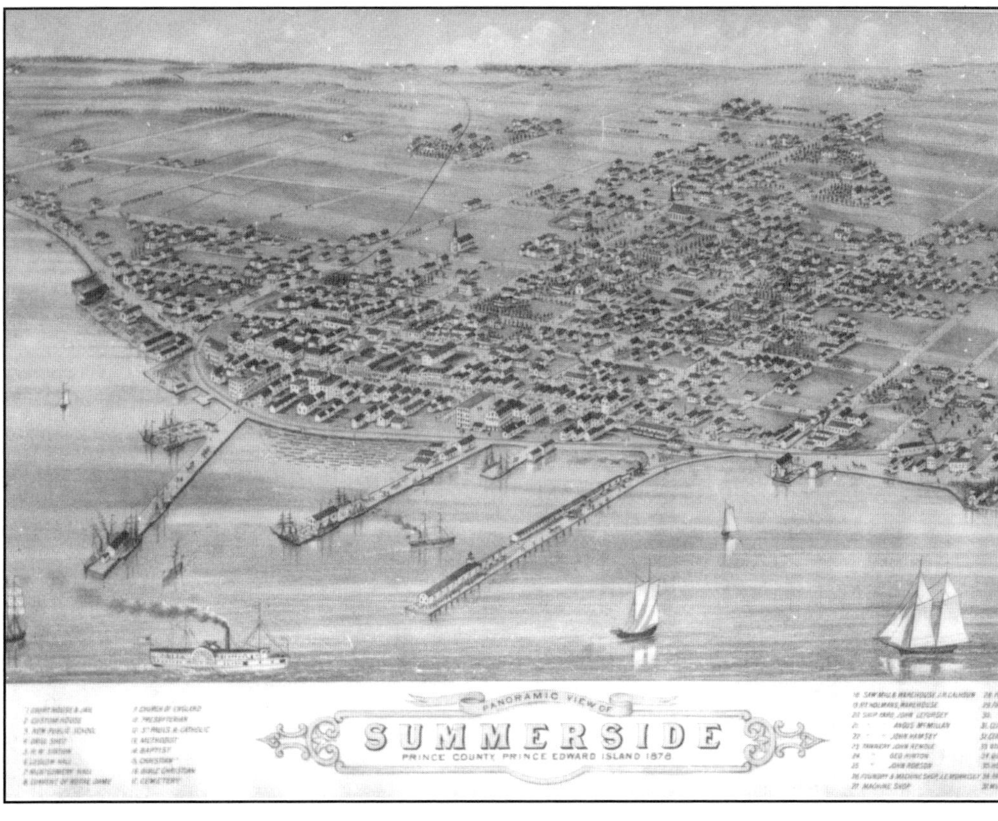

Led by shipbuilders such as Angus McMillan, William Richards, John LeFurgey, and J.C. Pope, transportation and shipbuilding were driving Summerside's economy. J.C. Pope could claim responsibility for half the vessels built in Bedeque Bay in the nineteenth century. Due to the impact of shipbuilding, by the 1880s Summerside was the commercial capital of Prince County and the western half of Prince Edward Island.

For many decades, wharves stretching out into the harbour welcomed incoming vessels carrying passengers and freight. Vessels making their way past the Indian Head Lighthouse, erected in 1881, and the breakwater, completed in 1909, glanced by Holman

The *Charles E. Lefurgey*, built by John Lefurgey in memory of his son. Launched in 1884, the 936-ton barque was the last of its size to be built at Summerside. By 1890, the industry had collapsed. Virtually all commercial sailing vessels had disappeared from the harbour by the late 1930s.

Island and docked safely at either the Queen, Holman, Railway, or Read wharves. After 1908, the water standpipe on Central Street, built atop the only hill in town, served as another landmark for vessel captains entering the harbour.

The late nineteenth-century economic phenomena that members of the Pope, Holman, Muirhead, and Lefurgey families took advantage of included a high demand for ships, reciprocity with the American states, a growing export trade in the raw products of farm and forest, the need for a shipping location closer than the Bedeque settlement to the entrance of the bay, and the introduction of steam and rail transportation. The legacy they left behind includes a mercantile market dominated by R.T. Holman Limited, one of the largest retail empires of the Maritimes, a number of manufacturing establishments, including the farm machinery pioneer Hall Manufacturing Company, and a service sector that supported a number of hotels, drugstores, and distributors of produce in the local Prince County market.

By the turn of the century, Summerside had grown into a vital transportation and industrial centre, surpassing all rivals for the title of largest and fastest-growing settlement in Prince County. Its population in the first year of the new century was 3,000—the

RIGHT: Fishermen wait on a Summerside wharf alongside the masts and rigging of their small fishing vessels, c.1910-20.

BELOW: On the shores of Bedeque Bay, barrels of oysters are hauled away to market, c.1900. Bedeque and Malpeque bays are renowned for oyster production.

second largest on Prince Edward Island—and development extended to the west, east, and north. The natural attributes of Summerside Harbour and Bedeque Bay served commercial, recreational, and practical roles throughout the twentieth century. Summerside's position on Northumberland Strait has guaranteed the impact of the bay and harbour on the everyday lives of the town's residents.

R.T. Holman Ltd. annual staff picnic at Cavendish Beach, 1932. This photo is particularly interesting because it incorporates both the Summerside staff and the staff from the Charlottetown branch store, established in 1923. It includes the matriarch of the family business, Ellen MacEwen Holman (1847-1938), wife of R.T. Holman.

The phrase "mercantile Summerside" rolls off the tongue of Summerside's early business leaders with a sense of confidence that belies the prosperity of this Maritime town. Although it later received a boost from the silver fox industry, Summerside was a merchant town from its beginning and it certainly remained so for the first seventy years of the twentieth century. Its role as a railway and steam service town played a part in its success, as did its strengths as a manufacturing and retail force.

In 1895, pioneer ranchers Robert Oulton and Charles Dalton raised the silver-black strain of foxes to maturity in captivity on Cherry Island in Cascumpeque Bay, west Prince County. The silver pelts returned as much as eighteen hundred dollars in London. By 1905 others who had been experimenting with fox breeding joined Oulton and Dalton and for a few years the secrets and the breeding stock remained in the hands of a group of six pioneers. Summerside was to play a vital part in the lucrative industry through a combination of luck, vision, and geography. Its entrepreneurial and transportation achievements served it well when the silver fox ranching industry set up its world headquarters in the town.

The outbreak of World War Two accelerated the decline of the silver fox industry just as the establishment of Royal Canadian Air Force (RCAF) station brought new economic life and energy to the town. Built in 1940 to address the Allies' need for trained aircraft crews to combat Nazi Germany, the air force base turned

Summerside into a military town, a development unforeseen at the start of the twentieth century. The base itself did not close until the early 1990s—but that is another story.

The social side of life in Summerside was connected to work life and the multitude of home-based tasks necessary for survival in a small, self-sufficient town. In short, there wasn't a lot of time for social life. Much fun was had on Sundays and Wednesday afternoons when workers were off, and founded as the community was on a seasonal agricultural economy, there were also seasonal breaks in the workload. The seasonal rhythm of life was as real in the 1930s and 40s as it had been in the 1880s and 90s.

Many of the young men who would lead Summerside through to the 1960s appear in the photograph on the following page, taken in the first decade of the twentieth century. The occasion for the meeting is unknown—various professionals and religious denominations are represented here. The group includes the man who would become the province's first Acadian premier, Aubin E. Arsenault, who as a young man practised law in Summerside.

Group of young men, c.1908.
FRONT ROW, l-r: **Athol MacLeod, Roy Holman, William Kennedy, Gus Bentley, Roy Silliphant.**
SECOND ROW: **Walter Lecky, Joe Duran, Leon Deagan, Hal Bowness, Robert Squarebriggs, Frank McInnis, Ed Dalton.**
THIRD ROW: **Wes MacDonald, Leonard McNeill, Joe MacDougall, Paul Durant, Frank Arnett, Howard Higgins, unidentified, (illegible) Cassidy.**
FOURTH ROW: **(illegible) McDonald, Hal Matthews, Camille Perry, Ed Reid, Harry Baker, A.E. Arsenault, Claude Phurp.**

The young gentlemen pictured in the photo appear ready to take on the new century. Disaster and opportunity by fire, ice, and war, great wealth from the silver fox, and a world without steamships, horse, and rail would all be apparent if not fully realized by the time the youngest among them had passed on.

Chapter 1

A Transportation Centre

SUMMERSIDE developed into an important transportation centre because of its location near the entrance to Bedeque Bay, the westernmost harbour of any size on the protected south side of Prince Edward Island. Proximity to the mainland rail connections made the town an attractive terminus for rail and steamship transportation from the 1860s onward. The dozen or more hotels in Summerside dating from the 1870s reflected its early role as a major transportation centre. When the impact of the new Borden to Cape Tormentine car ferry service (established in 1917) and the decline of the railway on Prince Edward Island challenged Summerside's stronghold on the island's movement of resources, Summerside responded by becoming a leading export centre for farm produce, especially potatoes, after about 1925.

This postcard from the early 1900s is entitled "Anticipation." Photo by W.S. Louson.

"Via Summerside: A Glance at the map will convince anybody that Providence had from the first ordained this place to be the gateway opening from all parts of the Island to the whole world outside."

THE CANADIAN TRADE REVIEW 1900

A Steamship Destination

Under the terms of Prince Edward Island's agreement to join the confederation of British North American colonies in 1873, the island was guaranteed "continuous communication" with the mainland. From its first years in Confederation, Summerside was a vital transportation link between the island and the mainland, and it remained at the centre of Prince Edward Island's steam communication with the outside world until 1917. A steamship service operated from Summerside to Point du Chêne, New Brunswick during the ice-free months. During the iced-in months—mid-December through March—small, open ice-boats left from Cape Traverse carrying essentials such as mail and a few hardy passengers who, out of necessity, travelled the nine miles in the face of unpredictable conditions. Although a winter boat service operated in the wider and deeper strait between Georgetown, Prince Edward Island and Pictou, Nova Scotia, most winters it was hindered by heavy ice. During the winter months, Summerside had to live without its shipping activity, and mail delivery and other basic services were dependent on the ice boats. The issue of transportation with the mainland constantly appeared in newspaper editorials of the first half of the century, especially into the 1930s and 1940s when the ferry service at Borden became better established.

Passengers on Summerside's Railway Wharf going between the steamer and the express train for Charlottetown, early 1900s.

The *St. Lawrence* and other late nineteenth-century paddle wheel steamers running regularly between Summerside and Pointe-du-Chêne, New Brunswick were succeeded by the *Princess*, the *Northumberland*, and, in 1906, the steel screw *Empress.*

Down at the Shore by Summerside historian Alan Rankin documents the importance of the steamship lines in the town's evolution. At the turn of the century, Summerside was a very busy harbour for both passengers and produce; four steamship companies provided Summerside with summer service. Every four days the beautiful *Campana* of the Quebec and Gulf Steamship

Sounds of the Town

***Pioneer* newspaper, Nov. 2, 1901:**

"The familiar howl of the SS *City of Ghent* was heard in the land yesterday at noon and, judging by the volume, her siren whistle is perfectly free from any taint of smallpox or other disease."

Company made a round trip between Quebec and the gulf ports. The Dobell Line *Polino* called at the town wharf on its way to Newfoundland, and the *City of Ghent* carried passengers and produce between Halifax and Summerside. *The Elliot* was a trading vessel running between Sydney, Nova Scotia and Summerside.

The backbone of the passenger service was the daily service across the thirty miles between Summerside and Pointe-du-Chêne (during the open months) provided by the Charlottetown Steam Navigation Company. According to *The Canadian Trade Review*, the company's steamer *Northumberland* was "palatial," measuring 225 feet in length, 33 feet in width, and 22 feet in depth, and capable of steaming at 16 knots. For passengers it had a "sumptuously appointed" saloon on deck. Upon arrival at the wharf, passengers found the Charlottetown train waiting to convey them to Charlottetown and "watering places and stations intermediate." For west-bound passengers, another train "backs down to the head of the landing pier a few minutes after the departure of the Charlottetown express."

Postcard of *Empress* docked at the Railway Wharf, c.1900.

Winter travel was something else altogether. From 1902 onward, *The Stanley* was used in early winter between Summerside and Cape Tormentine and in the Georgetown to Pictou run later in winter. Ice boats travelled the strait from Cape Tormentine to Cape Traverse not far from the entrance to Bedeque Bay until the early years of the twentieth century.

Important changes in travel occurred in 1917 with the advent of the car ferry service at Borden-Cape Tormentine. Passenger steamship service to Summerside became a thing of the past. For Summerside, the shift from steamship to ferry effected a major change in its provincial role and in its self-perception. No longer was Summerside the island's major rail-based link with the outside world.

The term "car ferry" originally referred to the ability to ferry rail cars across the Northumberland Strait. At the new terminal in Borden, the S.S. *Prince Edward Island* loads a motor vehicle via a flatbed rail car, which was the way all automobiles on the island traveled from 1917 to 1932. The system was cumbersome and did nothing to encourage motor travel.

Railroad Service

Prince Edward Island's entry into Confederation was secured by the promise to pay off the large railway debt it had incurred as it tried to build its own railway. After 1875, trains met the steamship passengers at the Railroad Wharf for passage to various island destinations. Freight service was also very important in the movement of primary materials, manufactured goods, and merchandise to fuel the retail sector.

The advent of the car ferry service meant the transference of winter transportation from the Georgetown-Pictou route to the Borden-Tormentine route. The new marine rail car service was an expression of the federal commitment to continuous transportation between Prince Edward Island and the mainland and a further fulfillment of the terms of Confederation.

Summerside was not an important railway town by accident. In the 1870s, residents fought to have the main line go through the town below Water Street, rather than around the town. The waterfront area was shared equally between rail and wharf. This configuration would change again with the increased emphasis on highway travel in the 1950s and 60s. The transition period, however, produced unusual images such as this one of the Clifton Hotel, probably taken by Lorne Read in the late 1930s.

CN 15952 Auto Railer, c.1938, in front of the Clifton Hotel.

In *A Photo History of the Prince Edward Island Railway*, Allan Graham identifies the photograph this way: "Auto-railer 15952 accepted by C.N.R. from the Evans Products Company of Detroit August 12, 1937." The third of only five trains manufactured, auto-railer 15952 carried twenty-five passengers and ended up as a road bus in Ontario.

Internal communication and transportation was difficult prior to the upgrading of roads and bridges that happened during the early years of the twentieth century. Bridges such as those at Bedeque and over the Wilmot—both built in the mid-1880s—combined to decrease the travel distance to Summerside by as much as four miles. Roads, however, were slow to improve; it would be the 1930s before the ferry service carrying passengers and freight between Summerside and Bedeque was no longer needed.

Jennie B. and the larger and more reliable *Wellington* were among the vessels serving the provincially subsidized Summerside-Lower Bedeque run. The last to serve was the fifty-foot *Venture "S,"* which was built and operated by Captain James Stright. It often carried potatoes into Summerside between passenger trips. By 1930 the service was intermittent and was finally terminated in 1938.

Social News

The Bedeque ferry was also used as a pleasure craft as this local news item from the *Summerside Pioneer* of August 3, 1901 confirms: "Capt. John L. Read entertained a number of friends with an enjoyable moonlight excursion on board his steamer, the *Frank C. Batt*, Thursday night. The boat steamed to Cape Tormentine and the party enjoyed the outing immensely."

The Hotels and Downtown

Late in September 1909 the *Summerside Journal* reported that the steamship *Empress* left Summerside with about 350 passengers on board, heavy traffic for so late in the season. The booming hotel business from the 1870s to the 1950s was directly connected to Summerside's role as a transportation centre.

Ida Green, Fanny Lecky, and Pearl McInnis on the Bedeque ferry, 1901.

Travellers needed places to stay overnight, so the Summerside of the late 1890s and early 1900s was a city of hotels. Among them were Campbell House, Terrace House, Strathcona Hotel, Queen Hotel, Clifton House, and Russ Hotel. The Queen Hotel was a new venture, having been established in 1899 by Acadian businessman Frank Perry, who renovated the old Doull furniture-manufacturing building at the base of Queen Street. Perry was the first successful businessman among the growing Acadian population of Summerside. Historian Ada MacLeod said it of the Queen, but it could be said of several hotels: "everything is designed to the public's liking, only twenty-one hours from Boston and twenty-six hours from New York and first class all the way."

On the north side of Water Street was Clifton House, pictured below, circa 1900. A postcard from about 1910 shows Central Street, which was around the east corner of the hotel. As the street name suggests, this corner was the centre of town in the early days and the location of the town's first store. It has been known variously as Clifton House corner, Strong's corner, and Pope's corner. In 1900 this was a thriving part of town, dominated

RIGHT: **Queen Hotel, est. 1899.**

"At the head of Queen's Wharf, convenient to the Quebec S.S. Company's landing place and the Bedeque Ferry, is the Queen's Hotel."

THE CANADIAN TRADE REVIEW 1900

BELOW: **Clifton House, c.1900.**

by the Summerside Journal building at the top of Queen Street, and Clifton House and Strong's store on the east side of Central Street. By this time Central Street was the route to the north shore, Malpeque Bay being only two miles to the north.

View up Central Street from Water Street, postcard, c.1910.

Chapter 2

World Headquarters of the Silver Fox Industry

THE FUR TRADE drew European interests ever deeper into continental North America from the sixteenth century onward. Native Americans traded animal skins and furs of all types for metals and manufactured European goods. Inevitably the wilderness areas changed: habitat disappeared and animal stocks became depleted or too difficult to reach by agents of the large fur-trading companies. Although the fur industry survived and prospered, efforts were continually being made to raise fur-bearing animals in captivity.

A number of Prince Edward Islanders were among those trying to raise animals for fur in captivity. They noticed that amongst the wild red fox population now and then black foxes with unusually beautiful silvery hairs would appear. The challenge taken up by several islanders, including B.I Rayner of Kildare, was to encourage this mutant silver strain through selective breeding in captivity. The fox farming industry began in the 1890s in western Prince Edward Island when Charles Dalton (1850-1933) and Robert Oulton (1835-1920) became partners and jointly established the first successful fox ranch on Cherry Island in Cascumpeque Bay. Oulton owned this property, and in its seclusion the first silver black foxes were successfully bred and their silver black offspring raised to maturity. The fur of the silver black fox became regarded as the "jewel" of the industry, not only because it was a thing of beauty, but also because it was rare.

The Big 6 Combine—Raising and Marketing in Secret

Between the 1890s and 1909, silver fox production was tightly controlled among six men who became known as the Big 6 Combine: Charles Dalton, Robert Oulton, B.I. and Silas Rayner, Robert Tuplin, and Captain James Gordon. Through the closely guarded sales of breeding stock among the six men, they independently achieved similar results within weeks or months of each other. For a time, they could not have known the real potential of their "industry," although they did resolve to guard their secrets carefully and it is widely believed that they had an agreement not to sell breeding stock outside their group.

Frank Tuplin, on the end of Combine 6 secrecy:

"When the outside world finds out about this there will surely be a tremendous stampede to get into the fox business and if these old ranchers won't sell foxes alive to the people, these animals won't be safe long in their unguarded pens."

With the covert actions of the cartel, the history of carefully controlled marketing of the silver fox had begun. The fox ranchers had good reason to protect their turf—news of terrific fur sales in London came to the island almost every year, and fox breeders outside the Big 6 Combine were trying to duplicate the group's breeding success in order to reap some of the profit for themselves. But time was not on the side of the Big 6—the veil of secrecy and resultant control of the industry were about to vaporize. It would be a few years before a semblance of carefully controlled marketing would return.

"In 1909 the understanding between the original owners, with reference to the sale of live foxes, ran out and the public soon became very much interested in a venture which seemed to promise such large proportionate returns" (*Summerside Journal*, 1916).

Frank Tuplin, a New Annan resident and Big 6 Combine partner, was under great pressure to sell a pair of breeders. He rationalized the sale of a pair of live silver foxes to George W. Robinson of Summerside by insisting that Robinson was merely a seventh member who had signed on by virtue of an agreement not to sell breeding stock for ten years. At the time Tuplin was a poor farmer and Robinson a miller; for the want of $5,000,

A fox in a pen at Rosebank Fur Farms, Prince Edward Island.

both the "gentleman's agreement" of the Big 6 Combine and a thirteen-year monopoly on island fox breeding stock came to an end. Pressure had been building on all the breeders, so after Tuplin's sale there was a flood of sales of breeding stock by other pioneer fox men.

H. T. Holman residence on Beaver Street in 1919. Holman's new home was similar in style and scale to his old home, which he had traded to newly rich fox rancher Frank Tuplin in 1911 for a pair of foxes valued at $15,000.

The years 1910-1914 were called the "fox boom," a period of economic expansion and speculation unsurpassed in Prince Edward Island's history. While the 1910 London fur sales signalled the start of the boom years, the impact in Summerside had to this point been minimal. Many individuals jumped into the industry, and people like Frank Tuplin became wealthy on breeding stock sales. Tuplin moved into H.T. Holman's house on Beaver Street, having purchased it from Holman for the price of two silver foxes, that is, $15,000. This in a time when a day's wage was a dollar or less! The great secrecy ended in part because many members were on the verge of large production. The "old ranchers" seemed no longer able to hold the lid on this industry. In fact, they might have feared not for themselves but for the safety of their animals.

The *Summerside Journal* of 1916 reported: "Probably the first Summerside people to take an interest in the business were Messrs. Roy and Harry Holman and John Hinton, who in the fall of 1910 purchased three pairs of foxes as the start of what is now known as the Park Farm Company." In 1925 H.T. Holman was referring to the ranch as Island Park Ranch (H.T. Holman diaries). In actual fact, many others, including the Callbeck family, were quite interested. Since the 1890s there had been knowledge of the workings of the Big 6 Combine, so others were ready to join in, having experimented on their own. "About this time also, the Willow Hill Company was formed by Messrs. Howatt, Locke, Manson, Monkley and Scales, who purchased one pair of foxes from Mr. B.I. Rayner. This company has been wonderfully prosperous having paid as high as 1,000% in cash [dividends] in a single year" (*Summerside Journal,* 1916). E.W. Manson was at the centre of the Willow Hill operation. Another well-known rancher from the boom years was B. Graham Rogers. The industry spread quickly to all parts of the island. People went to the woods in search of silver foxes, dubbed "free gold" by rancher B.I. Rayner Jr. The mere sight of a fox track in the snow or on the ground would send the whole neighbourhood into a chase for a prize worth anywhere from $500 to $1000, depending upon the pelt. The fact that hardly a fox of any variety could be found while the boom was on is reflected in the seemingly tongue-in-cheek postcard of "black beauties" and their vaulted home in the O'Leary area of Prince County.

Postcard of a fox vault. Is it real or the editorial work of a playful photographer? In either case, it sums up the spirit of the fox boom.

International Headquarters: Summerside

Summerside was the established mercantile centre for western Prince Edward Island and an important transportation and export centre, so it was a natural location for fox buyers and sellers to gravitate to. Local entrepreneurs gladly took the lead in the industry. With the arrival in Summerside of the Canadian National Silver Fox Breeders Association (CNSFBA) in 1920, followed by the Dominion Experimental Fox Ranch (DEFR) in 1925, the town's position as industry leader was cemented. The CNSFBA emerged from the desire to establish a registration system for fox pedigree, and the DEFR represented the federal government's commitment to research and development in the industry.

The great world markets for furs were located in large urban centres of trade and industry such as London, New York, and Montreal, where wholesalers purchased practically all of the Prince Edward Island furs. Despite the long distances from Prince Edward Island to these marketing centres, the production costs

Models at an international show modelling furs from Canada, c.1955.

BELOW:
Experimental Fox Ranch located on Central Street at the north extremity of the town from 1925.

were relatively small in relation to the value of the commodity. On the island, a prosperous mixed farming industry combined with favourable geographic conditions created a highly successful fox farming industry. In fact it was believed that island silver foxes, in part because surrounded by water and cut off from the mainland, had developed into a distinct, high quality sub-species of that colour variety. True or not, the argument was no doubt useful to clever marketers.

The involvement of Summerside people in the fur industry changed it forever; in turn, Summerside would never be the same —it became the international headquarters for the silver fox business, and home of the most glamourous fur worldwide in the era of longhair fur fashion. In demand by the world's wealthiest

Glamour photo of Canadian Fur Salon Show at L'institute France-Canada, Paris, one of the finest collections of Canadian fur ever assembled by the Canadian government for display in Europe.

people, the silver fox fur was considered the richest fur in the world. It was to Summerside what the sable was to Russia.

"Summerside was the capital for the industry—no question about that," says long-time fox rancher and industry leader Lloyd Lockerby of nearby Hamilton, Prince Edward Island. "From an economic point of view the fox industry over a couple of decades built the town." Lockerby makes the point that no other world-wide industry started here. World headquarters were usually in large metropolitan centres such as London and New York, whereas in the case of the silver fox, the world headquarters was in Summerside and its branch offices were in London and New York.

Lloyd Lockerby, long-time fox rancher of Hamilton, PEI:

"Summerside was the capital for the industry—no question about that. From an economic point of view the fox industry over a couple of decades built the town."

In the 1920s demand for the silver fox fur was "fantastic," said Lockerby. Anyone who wanted livestock had to go to Summerside to get it.

SATELLITE INDUSTRIES

Summerside's economy was affected by the fur boom at every level, from primary production to processing, marketing, and service and support industries—not to mention research and development, industry lobby, administration, and governance. The benefits of economic growth spread throughout the local economy. During the boom years, the excitement, fame, and fortune were unprecedented. The war dampened the industry for a time, but it re-kindled immediately afterward so that the 1920s were exceptionally good years, with the demand for livestock continuing at a feverish pace. Shipments started to go to the United States, Scandinavian countries, and farther afield.

Fox ranchers had to build ranches, so local companies benefitted from large contracts. And the increased demand for lumber and building materials meant that the silver fox industry was good for the construction industry. The Summerside Ranching Company and the Saunders Ranch were two major jobs won by the M.F. Schurman Company. In fact, the fox business accounted for nearly fifty per cent of the company's work in the 1920s. Lumber and other construction materials were needed for pens, fences, and barns, not to mention housing for newly made millionaires!

The CNSFBA, the Prince Edward Island Fur Pool, and others who sold insurance to shipping agents profited to a degree they could never have imagined. Reg Ellis credited the fox industry, namely the volume of insurance on the storage buildings where the pelts were stored, with helping him get his insurance business started.

1937 The complete line of SunGlo fox and animal foods.

Lowell Hancock's International Fox and Animal Foods building on First Street, Summerside.

Sun-Glo Feed, the fox feed company started by Lowell Hancock, sold products throughout the Maritimes. Active on the executive of the CNSFBA, Hancock also owned Ohio National Ranch and International Fox and Animal Foods Limited. Brace McKay and Company—one of the largest outlets for fox industry equipment—supplied the wire used for fox pen construction and

A measure of the abundance of the fox industry: fox biscuits piled high on Brace's truck, 1936.

other kinds of hardware. The wire was imported from England and retailed in Summerside and other North American locales.

Other companies diversified to meet the demand. Hall Manufacturing Company, established in the 1860s by Thomas Hall, was primarily a farm machinery manufacturer whose product was recognized as superior at the Dominion Exhibitions in the 1880s and 90s. Hall Manufacturing fended off competition from central Canada by limiting production to a few select lines manufactured locally and by selling carefully selected imports. Besides plows, diggers, mowers, and reapers, the company was perhaps best known for its Eureka fanning mill, which separated the grain from the chaff and was manufactured until the 1920s. By the twentieth century the main business location for Hall Manufacturing was a cluster of large barns and warehouses on the north side of Water Street East, to the east of M.F. Schurman Company. To meet the fox fur industry head-on, Hall diversified into cold storage, bringing in frozen fox feed, most of it fish. Hall's cold storage was in a building separate from the manufacturing plant. The spring of 1925 appears to have been an especially good year, as H.T. Holman's diary entry read:

> MAY 4 *Hall Co. running continuously these days freezing herring. Rooms both storeys almost full now with customers and companies, meat and fish.*

May 9 *RBC demand loans some $19,000 less than last year. April sales some 19,000 ahead of last year. Lobster fishing reported fairly good on Northside. Hall Co. has finished taking herring, have about 60 tons for selves and customers representing about 2000 paid out to S'side fishermen within the last two weeks—cold storage is absolutely full.*

Another contingent to serve the industry was the pharmacy, which sold flea powders, ear mite powders, and worm pills, among other products. The pharmacies of the day included Boates', Enman's, Foley's, and Gourlie's.

Storefront at Holman's featuring prizes won by Summerside ranchers. Trophies like these would have adorned the mantels and offices of many leading fox breeders.

Two individuals who made significant contributions to the fox industry after World War One were Peter G. Clark and George A. Callbeck, both of Summerside. Under the auspices of his Canadian Silver Black Fox Company, established in 1912, Clark developed the legendary pure Canadian or "Canuck" line of foxes, a consistent winner at the Royal Winter Fair in Toronto. Clark was a charter member of the CNSFBA, but in 1929 he and a few others broke away and established a competitor—the Prince Edward Island Fur Pool. Besides taking fox pelts on consignment, the organization also featured a feed supply division and field services.

George Callbeck became a legend in fox-farming circles. He worked with his father, who experimented with breeding as early as 1905 and was strongly committed to the industry during the boom years. By 1916 George A. Callbeck was manager of the Willow Hill Ranch and by 1921 he was in partnership with B. Graham Rogers. In 1926 he struck out on his own, forming the Royal Ranch, which consisted of thirty acres on the north end of Granville Street in Summerside. This ranch would serve as an industry showplace. The exotic-sounding silvers, platinums, and glacier-blue platinums raised there brought championships to the ranch from 1925 until 1962, when Callbeck retired from fox ranching.

The silver fox industry was one of the highlights of life in Summerside during the twentieth century. It helped protect the town from the worst ravages of the Depression and provided the agricultural community with a ready cash source to complement other ventures. The arrival of World War Two and a shift in tastes among fur buyers worldwide finally brought the silver fox era to an end. The legacy of the industry's fame and fortune may be seen today in the built heritage harking back to the illustrious fox era, and in the museum and hall of fame devoted to the industry.

The wealth gained from the silver fox industry aided greatly in the replacement of beautiful homes lost to the "Great Fire" of 1906. Summerside's enviable architectural heritage survives to this day. In 1915, this home on Central Street was built for about $1,400—a mere fraction of the value of one of fox rancher and businessman H.G. Muttart's foxes.

Chapter 3

Fire and War

AS IN MANY other towns of nineteenth- and early twentieth-century Canada, fire in Summerside was a frightful threat to the well-being of the community and a common cause of property loss. After two major fires, one in 1906 and one in 1916, Summerside resembled cities devastated by the Great War. As it battled against fire on the home front, the town responded to the call for volunteers to defend the British Empire overseas. What many thought would be a tour of a few months—some left in August thinking they would be back by Christmas—turned into an extended nightmare, one far from the peaceful surrounds of Bedeque Bay. Several hundred did not return. For those who did, the town was a changed place.

Summerside, like most wooden towns of the period, was constantly challenged by the threat of fire. In 1867 the Summerside firefighting and prevention brigade was reorganized in the wake of other major town fires in the Maritime colonies. At this time every property owner was required by law to have a bucket readily available in case of fire. Later in the nineteenth century, there were a number of fires, ranging in seriousness from the Central Street fire of 1884, which consumed a whole block, to those that took individual businesses only. In 1886 the town's first steam fire engine arrived. In 1896 the headquarters of the *Journal Pioneer* newspaper burned for a second time. The building was replaced immediately, this time in brick, and stands today as one of the oldest extant commercial sites in Summerside.

The Great Fire of 1906

Ten years later, a fire since unmatched devastated Summerside. As recently as October 1905 the town had been reminded by the *Summerside Journal* that its water works were not "in order." A fire drill showed that it would take eighteen minutes for the steam-powered fire engine to gather enough steam to start pumping water—long enough for even the largest brick building to be gutted. But very little could have been done to prepare for the fire on October 10, 1906, a tragic day in Summerside history. By the time the fire was over the next day, over one hundred houses had been lost, as had a sizable portion of the downtown business sector. Fortunately no human lives were taken.

A before and after set of images shows the northwest section of town, between Summer and Central streets, from the vantage point of the post office. Among the easily identifiable buildings in the "before" image are the Anglican church (with square belfry) in the centre and the rectory (with turret) in the lower left. The building on the lower right is believed to be the Russ Hotel, which burned; behind it is Willard Hall, which also burned. The gabled house with the diamond-shaped attic window survived, and today is owned by the Clark family. It is in the same location on the edge of Memorial Square.

Looking northwest from the post office before the 1906 fire (below) and after (bottom).

The "after" image, with its view from roughly the same angle, offers us an appreciation of the fire's sheer destruction: the courthouse stands alone where only the day before more than twelve buildings stood.

It is believed that a spark from one of the engines in the busy railway yard ignited one

end of the wooden freight shed sometime before 10:00 P.M. A strong wind from the southeast made the fire impossible to control, despite the concerted efforts of both the Summerside and Charlottetown firefighters. Burning cinders blew over town, and the fire, hindered only by open squares, made its way through the prime residential section of town.

Contemporary newspaper accounts and subsequent historians have described the horror of that night. Lost in the fire were many town landmarks such as the Strathcona Hotel, the Baptist,

Map of Summerside showing the path of the fire.

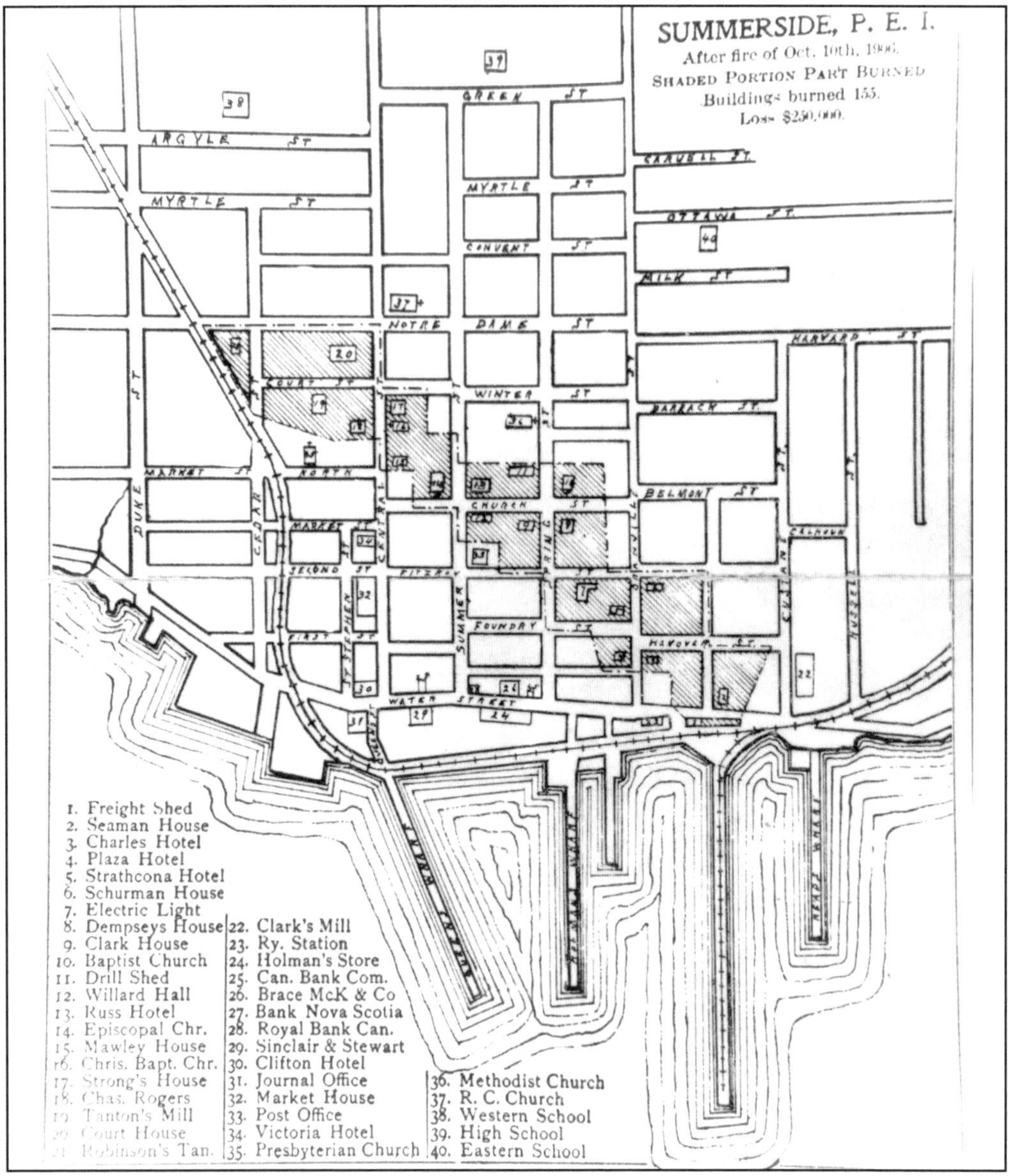

ABOVE: **The Christian Church on Central Street, lost in the fire of 1906.**

BELOW: **View to the northeast prior to the fire of 1906, with the Baptist church in centre of photo.**

Anglican, and Christian churches, many residences—Will Strong's house, for instance, and businesses such as Tanton's Mill and Robinson's Tannery. The courthouse was gutted, although the walls, which were left standing, were used in its restoration. Because the courthouse was a large two-storey brick building, it played a crucial role in shielding the houses beyond it. Heavy rain at dawn helped the firefighters, who included in their numbers volunteers that came by special train from Charlottetown.

The view to the east was no more encouraging. The Baptist church on the corner of Spring and Church streets is the centrepiece of this "before" view to the northeast (below). Behind it stands the Lefurgey house, which did not burn; however, all the buildings between it and the camera, including the church, were consumed. From the post office to the southeast, the Electric Light Plant chimney still stands, with nothing but a pile of rubble at its base. Beyond the chimney on Fitzroy Street is where the Charles, Plaza, and Strathcona hotels once stood. The latter was perhaps the most

LEFT: The Strathcona Hotel in 1900, not long after it was constructed. It was lost in the 1906 fire.

BELOW: Electric Light Plant chimney viewed from the post office after the 1906 fire.

impressive and had been in existence for only a few years. In the language of the time, it offered "attractions as a handsome, quiet, well kept and altogether reputable house."

The magnitude of this disaster was staggering, destroying as it did most of the residential core of the town. On the other hand, it fuelled a construction boom that lasted for years. A number of contractors were instrumental in rebuilding the hundred or more structures that were destroyed. The *Summerside Journal* writes in 1908: "Summerside is a busy place this summer. Labourers and artisans have no difficulty in securing employment. M.F.

The M.F. Schurman Company sash and door factory and planing mill, c.1910.

Schurman and Company have a number of contracts on hand and about fifty men are employed on the buildings in course of erection." Three years after the fire, the October 13, 1909 issue of the newspaper reported that over fifty new buildings, including three new churches, had been constructed.

The courthouse was rebuilt by contractors P.G. Clark and D.R. Morrison in 1908. M.F. Schurman Company, newly re-located to the east end of town at the Clarks Mills location on the corner of Eustane and Water streets, would secure lucrative contracts around the Maritimes throughout the century.

New Water Works

It took the disastrous fire of 1906 to convince the town of the need for a civic water works. The new water works went into operation on September 14, 1908, under the management of commissioners T.B. Grady, Hon. James A. MacNeill, and J.S. Hinton. This photo from about 1950 shows the water standpipe on

Trask Drilling Company at the second town water standpipe, c.1950.

Central Street, in the same general location as the first and the two succeeding standpipes—atop the town's highest hill. The first standpipe, rising 125 feet above ground and measuring 25 feet in diameter, served as a visual locator for incoming planes. It was painted orange and black to match the buildings of the new Summerside Airport, built in 1934.

The Great War 1914-1918

Once displaying its loyalty to the British Empire by participating in the Boer War, the island showed its support again by participating in the next major conflict: The Great War. The Prince County Patriotic Recruiting Society led the charge. Eleven Summerside men became part of the "B" Squadron 36th Prince Edward Island Light Horse Regiment headquartered in the town. Summerside men fought in the 2nd Siege Battery and the 2nd Heavy Battery.

Families pitched in when they could. Fitzroy Street resident Jeremiah Noonan, named after an ancestor from County Tipperary, Ireland, was the patriarch of a musical family that responded to the war effort by offering musical services at patriotic events across the province. The Great War hit Summerside forcefully, causing a period of economic stagnation. The exact number of Summerside men to serve overseas is not known, but more than three hundred men from Prince County did not return. The war brought visible changes to the town: a new barracks was erected,

The Red Cross Spinners of Summerside made clothing to send overseas. Soldier C. Mountain noted "how a little kindness from the folks back home helps the boys to carry on...."

the Crystal Rink became a shooting range in summer, and the Happyland Theatre showed valiant military documentaries to boost home morale. There were fewer young men at dances and other social events, and some residents swore off liquor for the duration of the war. Older residents of the town, such as the late Herb Schurman, recalled late in the war seeing German POWs marched through the town to the train station on their way to the rail and ferry terminal construction sites at Borden.

A number of skilled artisans were required at the front, not the least of which was the farrier-blacksmith. One volunteer whose memorabilia is cherished by family in Summerside was Farrier Sergeant John E. O'Connor of Cape Traverse. In the summer of his 46th year, O'Connor knew he was needed at the front—so he left, expecting to be home by Christmas. One newspaper of the day describes his departure in the most emphatic of recruiting terms: "Another patriotic Islander—Mr. John E. O'Connor, late mail driver of Cape Traverse—is one of the patriotic sons who has shown his devotion to duty in defence of the Grand Old Flag by resigning a very lucrative position as blacksmith for the Rogers Miller Company at

Sounds of the Town

Ruth Noonan and Zeta Durant put their piano lessons to use by playing and singing at patriotic rallies, part of the campaign to gather and recruit island boys. Songs like "There Will Always Be an England," "God Save The King," "Never Let the Old Flag Fall," "Rule Britannia," and "Keep the Home Fires Burning" indicated that this was a war to be fought on behalf of the old Empire. Entertainers went by horse and buggy and train across the countryside as newspapers of the day proclaimed: "Be a Man! Get into Khaki."

Horse artillery, unidentified front, 1918. Photo by Jack Turner of O'Leary, PEI.

Carleton Point as well as severing the dearest ties that bind a good man to his home, that of leaving behind him to anxiously await his safe return, a faithful wife and daughter."

On the remote battlefields of Europe, Summerside was making its contribution. Arthur Corney, for example, received Belgium's highest medal of honour for deeds of bravery. Not only did Corney permanently injure his hands in the war, but the horror of it left him unable to talk about his experiences. Corney was the father of Summerside resident and historian Frances (Corney) Lakhan.

Jack Turner, who served four years in the artillery, including two and a half years on the front lines, hid his camera and recorded the war from the ordinary soldier's perspective. He was present at Ypres, the Somme, and Vimy. His many photos are part of the holdings of the Public Archives of Prince Edward Island.

Close to Vimy after the ridge was taken in 1917. Photo by Jack Turner.

Guy Rodd, Brackley, describes the Front

Speaking sixty years later, 2nd Siege Battery member Guy Rodd of Brackley, Prince Edward Island describes the impact of war on the senses and the constant craving for optimism: "I hope I am not putting out the worst side of it, but you asked me a question…The stench of death, of dead soldiers, dead horses, and you know in an advance you just couldn't bury everything at once and in hot weather—I think you could imagine just what it would be like. Well then of course on top of that we had gas put over by shells—later in the war. When the sun would come out, those things would start and you would realize that you were getting more gas than you should be. Along with tear gas—that miserable darn thing wouldn't kill you but you can weep a lot over it. And cordite, which is used for powder. There was always the smell, the stench of pollution, I don't know how people would live under it today [laughter]. Those were the conditions which you were subject to all the time! [We] lived underground for approximately three years. And of course in those three years you see a lot and you learn a lot and you commence to get the feeling that, well, "I guess I am not going to go for a little while yet!"

Devastation at the battle of the Somme, Longueual (Deville Wood), 1916. Photo by Jack Turner.

The Summerside boys joined other islanders of the 2nd Siege Battery daily wondering if their "number would come up." For some, it did. For the others, when finally the sun did shine on a peaceful Europe, they joined their comrades and returned home to a resounding welcome. The Victory Parade proceeded east on Water Street past a streetscape that included several nineteenth-century buildings and the Clifton Hotel. In 1916, fire had devoured a large portion of the downtown business sector, most of it to the east of the location pictured below.

Military victory parade at the west end of Water Street, in front of the Clifton Hotel, c.1919.

The Fire of 1916—the business district takes a devastating hit

On December 16, 1916, a fire started in the basement of the Sinclair and Stewart building. Through hard work and good fortune, the fire was eventually confined to the block between Water, Summer, First, and Central streets. Still, the damage was costly, totalling $400,000 in commercial property losses. The fire of 1906 was less costly as it was mostly residential property that was lost.

In some cases the fires of both 1906 and 1916 created open spaces—but at a very dear price. The fires did not have a great impact on the geography or street layout in the town; however, sadly, significant architecture of the shipbuilding era was lost forever. Perhaps the outstanding example is the Sinclair and Stewart enterprise, which was housed within the late nineteenth-century Crabbe Block on the south side of Water Street. Undaunted, the town quickly commenced re-building. By the 1930s there were few open spaces left, as can be seen in the aerial view of the town in chapter five.

Photographer Lorne H. Read of Read's Studio recorded an impressive series of images that shows the extent of the damage. Virtually all were made into postcards—a popular practice during the 1910s. The first image, taken from near the corner of

At centre stands the Royal Bank on Water Street. Unscathed and to the right are the buildings of Queen Street—at extreme right, the part of the Journal Pioneer Building occupied today by Williams and Crue is visible. Also at right, the fourth storey of the Queen Hotel rises above other Queen Street buildings.

First and Summer streets, is to the south and shows only the Royal Bank of Canada left standing in that block. To the left of the bank stand the gates that once opened onto Joe Locke's Ice Cream Parlour.

Harry MacGougan, son of William Keir MacGougan, one of the principals of MacGougan and Wright, was an eyewitness to the 1916 fire: "I was five when Sinclair and Stewart burned, and saw the fire from our attic window on Winter Street. We thought the whole town would go." He also noted that it was unfortunate that Percy Bowness' picture studio was gutted as "they had a number of pictures of Summerside."

The Holman water tower partly explains how the Holman complex was saved. With water from the tower and its own hoses, the Holman company was able to prevent the fire from igniting the store, stopping the fire with just two buildings to spare. In the succeeding days, residents, including the man atop the Royal Bank at left in the bottom photo, came out to survey the damage. The women at left in the photo are standing on Strong's corner, where the F.W. Strong general store had been.

Summerside lawyer Ned Wyatt wrote to his daughter on December 18, 1916 describing the fire from his vantage point on Spring Street, across from the Methodist church: "There was great havock [sic]...Mother was in bed but with the wind blowing a gale in our direction she got up and helped pack up and took the law registers and had them in the hall for a grand rush in case it spread. Fortunately it did not come further."

RIGHT: View to the south from the corner of Central and First streets. Freestanding walls in the distance are all that remain of the Sinclair and Stewart building and the Crabbe Block. Left foreground may be the remnants of the Bowness Photography Studio.

BELOW: Townsfolk survey the damage. The Holman water tower is visible at far right in this view to the east on Water Street.

Immediately after the fire, businesses took up temporary housing: "Sinclair & Stewart have their office in the Town house building next to the Journal[,] for groceries…Dalton's in Clifton where the fox exchange was." Sinclair and Stewart's new building was a dramatic change in style, though it took little time to build.

Sinclair and Stewart's replacement store, c.1918.

The fires of both 1906 and 1916 spawned a mini-industry in souvenir images in the popular postcard format of the day. Harry Holman and Miss Gladys Holman were frequent customers at the Read Studio, where for the period July 1916 to June 1917 the ledger reads: "Margaret in Scotch costume, 4 fox pictures, 8 pictures of fire (post cards), 3 photos of auto group—total $33.25." It is clear what the year would be remembered for.

Above: **View looking east on Water Street before the 1916 fire, with Gourlie's, Sinclair and Stewart, and the Crabbe Block on the right (south side of street) and, barely visible at left, the Royal Bank and Joe Locke's Ice Cream Store, c.1914. Note Gourlie's Prince County Drugstore, right foreground, bought by pharmacist J.E. Dalton in 1913.**

Below: **After the 1916 fire, smouldering ruins are all that were left of the streetscape above.**

The theme of great fires and how they were fought is a strong one for the town. Newspaper photographer George Wotton worked for the *Guardian* in the 1950s. Anytime a fire alarm sounded at the fire hall, a general siren would alert the volunteer force—the cue for the newspaper to call the fire hall for details. On February 2, 1955, Wotton heard the siren and called the department; all he got was a terse "here" and a click of the receiver. The fire hall was attached to the town hall, which was ablaze! Town records, wet but salvageable, were eventually removed from the vault by John Cameron and Harry Dye.

Smoke billows from the eves and windows as the town hall is destroyed by fire in February 1955, as recorded by Don Sears of Read Studio.

City officials John Cameron and Harry Dye rescue slightly damaged town records from the vault after it cooled down.

BELOW: The exterior shell of the town hall, with the fire hall now detached, is all that remains the day after.

Guardian photographer George Wotton captures the interior view of the ruined town hall, February 1955.

Chapter 4

The RCAF Station and Post-war Summerside

WORLD WAR TWO had a far greater impact upon the town of Summerside than did World War One; it created jobs in Prince County, stimulated local industry, and, most significantly, created another source of long-term prosperity: the RCAF Summerside Station. Predictably, the response to the war among the young men of the area was positive, and the Prince Edward Island Highlanders were the first to mobilize. Indeed, in the fall of 1939, mobilization was happening everywhere.

In an area where local telephone service had been initiated only a decade earlier, new technologies brought the war closer to home. Commercial radio for home entertainment arrived in the 1920s, but in the 1930s, with short wave radio, it was possible for

Mobilized Prince Edward Island Highlanders leave Summerside aboard the Holman truck, 1939.

operators, even teenaged ones like Davis Green, to make their own ham radios and speak to operators in South America and Europe. Meanwhile, aircraft flight was becoming more common in the industrialized world, and the craft larger and more sophisticated. Lorne Read of Read Studio was on the scene when one of Italian dictator Mussolini's planes was forced to land in Victoria Harbour.

The RCAF Station Comes to Summerside

Margaret MacFarlane's history of the M.F. Schurman Company traces the chain of events leading to the creation of the air force training base in St. Eleanors, just north of Summerside: "On April 4, 1940, the cabinet of Prime Minister MacKenzie King announced that Canada had been selected to host the British Commonwealth Air Training Program and on May 2, 1940 the federal government announced that Prince Edward Island would be part of the program." The newly appointed Minister of National Defence was Colonel Ralston, a parachuted candidate invited by the prime minister to return to politics and run in Prince County—the same constituency that King himself had successfully parachuted into a little more than a decade before—where he was duly elected.

Returning home from the World's Fair in Chicago in 1936, an aircraft from the famous Italian air armada encountered engine trouble and had to make an emergency landing at Victoria Harbour.

Under the British Commonwealth Air Training Plan of 1940-45, military bases were planned for Mt. Pleasant, Wellington, and St. Eleanors. At St. Eleanors, airmen would be trained for overseas duty. The plan was to operate Mt. Pleasant and Wellington mainly as alternative landing fields should the St. Eleanors (Summerside) airfield be too busy or unapproachable.

Airport construction began in July 1940. *Forty Years 1941-1981: A History of the Base at Summerside* states that "the main aerodrome at St. Eleanors was to have two hard-surfaced runways each 2,500 feet long and 75 feet wide. Curran and Briggs of St. Eleanors was awarded the contract for the construction of the airfield. Long lines of trucks awaited their turn with a large diesel shovel. Three scoops, five tons of Prince Edward Island farm soil, and the truck was on its way. Three graders worked around the clock leveling the runways and taxiways."

Increased commercial activity, employment, new people for the community, and jobs for locals were all part of this unique opportunity. For the construction contract winners—M.F. Schurman Company Limited—it was a defining moment. Nine months would pass and the company "would erect thirty-two buildings, including five hangars, a military hospital, office headquarters, barracks, garages and machine shops, on a site covering approximately forty-five acres"(*Forty Years*). At peak construction there were 410 people on the payroll. Before the year was out,

An aerial view of tarmac area, Summerside Station, c.1944. #1 Navigational School was operating at this time, so there are approximately fifty Anson aircraft visible in this photo. A four-engine Liberator and six Canso Flying Boats—which patrolled for submarines in Maritime waters at this time—are visible too.

there were four more military buildings, including a guardhouse and administration building at the Summerside military base. The military base project was immense, total freight being enough to fill 1,130 freight cars, more than would fit on the nine miles of railway track from Kensington to Summerside.

The economic impact from construction of the base was just the first of its effects. Military training activity continued after the war, evolving into anti-submarine patrols in the late fifties and into the sixties. Summerside's mostly fog-free location in the central southern Gulf of St. Lawrence made it ideal for the search and rescue services established there in the late 1960s. For Prince Edward Islanders, Maritimers, and Canadians from all parts of the country, Summerside had become a military town. Because of the British Commonwealth Air Training Plan at Summerside and points west, advertising images such as this lantern slide from R.T. Holman Limited shown at the local Capitol Theatre had special significance.

During the war years, Summerside was the home of two separate outfits. The first was No. 9 Service Flying Training School (No. 9 SF15). "The primary purpose of the school was to provide further training to pilots coming from Elementary Flying Training in order to prepare them for operational flying positions overseas. The first course of 56 pilots started on January 6, 1941, receiving their wings some four months later" (*Forty Years*). In total, two hundred pilots from around the commonwealth learned to fly in Summerside.

This slide beckons the movie-goer to come into Holman's for a demonstration of the new Symbol of Air Supremacy—the 1941 RCA Victor Globetrotter, Model A-32.

In July 1942, on the heels of the departing Service Flying Training School, the No. I General Reconnaissance School (No. 1 GRS) commenced operation at Summerside. Reconnaissance training was needed to combat the German submarine threat. "They ran courses for both pilots and navigators. Flying was conducted in the twin-engine ANSON. The course length was nine weeks for pilots and four weeks for navigators. A new course started every week so that by mid-May in 1944 there were 576 aircrew continuously undergoing training. By the summer of 1944 a total of 6,004 aircrew had been trained at No. 1 GRS. This total included 3,412 pilots, 2,400 navigators (bombardier) and 192 navigators (wireless)" (*Forty Years*). While this schedule caused severe overcrowding most of the time, the base managed to cope. The final change before war's end occurred in February of 1945 when the school was renamed No. 1 Reconnaissance and Navigation School and basic air navigation was added to the curriculum.

Although it may not have been apparent at the time, Summerside changed irrevocably when the military moved in. Suddenly there was an old and a new community—the small Summerside town and the new military base—existing side by side in all their differences. What the military found in Summerside was open arms and hearts. Long-time residents recall no animosity between townspeople and military personnel, despite a fundamental difference between them: the locals were there to stay and the military personnel were transient, sometimes transferred at

First Wings Parade at No. 9 SFTS 1941 with Prince County MP and Minister of National Defence Colonel Ralston on the stand addressing those assembled.

short notice. From the outset, Summerside was an excellent host to Canadian and visiting fighting forces.

A whole new community was now on Summerside's doorstep. Personnel came to Summerside by the busload from Mt. Pleasant for evening entertainment, while others moved in—if married, they rented downtown, if single, they lived on the base. Awash with military people from outside the community, Summerside had to adjust socially.

Anson aircraft in the early morning line-up, c.1942. They took to the air daily as soon as possible.

In the rural area, where the base was located, intense construction activity followed by four years of war made a strong impact upon what had been a quiet, rural community. "The Harvards filled the air" and Charlie Tanton remembers seeing a dozen or so overhead and landing on recently converted farmland. The Tanton family was one of a number of families required to sell their farm at St. Eleanors to make way for the RCAF base. In fact, most of rural North St. Eleanors was gobbled up by the airport.

Beyond the remarkable construction period, there were ongoing employment opportunities for many islanders in fields such as maintenance, mechanical instruction, and various service contracts.

RIGHT: Mechanics instructor Bob Dewar of Summerside, second from right sitting on the wing, with some of his students.

Wings Parade, June 19, 1942. Group captain Fullerton pins wings on Sergeant J.J. Sebisty of Hamilton, Ontario.

World War Two

In Summerside, the patriotic rhetoric for World War Two was not as strong as it had been for The Great War. Only during the Victory Loan campaigns was there an attempt at drumming up patriotic fervour. Summerside journalist Elmer Murphy wrote in his memoirs: "All kinds of gimmicks were used to put a loan over the top, and we dutifully reported them all and, as I recall, in all cases the island communities over subscribed their quotas." Etched in the minds of youngsters like George Key Jr. was the image published in the newspaper of the MacNeill Family, four brothers all marching smartly in uniform, paired with a call to buy Victory Bonds.

The Armoury with Victory Loan signs.

Summerside sent its fair share of residents off to war; in fact, the war robbed the town of a good percentage of a generation of young men. Of those who returned, some found themselves back in school to finish their grades—quite a challenge as they were by now four or five years older than their classmates and worlds apart in

Victory Arch at the foot of Summer Street—buy Victory Bonds and drive the dagger into the heart of Hitler!

experience. Victory in Europe or "VE" Day was a day of jubilation. The image at the bottom of this page records the victory parade as it proceeded down Summer Street. Note the retailer vendors or liquor store—referred to simply as the vendors—on the east side of the street and the town hall in the centre background of the photo.

The McNeill boys—l-r: Ronald J. McNeill, Hubert B. McNeill, D. Tanton McNeill, and Francis J. McNeill—of the Prince Edward Island Highlanders go off to war in kilts. From the Halifax *Chronicle Herald*, Dartmouth, c.1939. The lads were four of the twelve children of Daniel and Pearl McNeill of Summerside. Three other siblings also joined services for the war.

BELOW: VE Parade down Summer Street.

A Post-War Future

Because of the air force base (and despite its being much more than a single industry town), Summerside became known in the Maritimes as a military town. With the war over, there was reason to doubt the future of the base; however, the issue was resolved in Summerside's favour when in 1947 it was announced that RCAF Station Summerside would be reactivated as a permanent peace-time installation. Between 1947 and 1953, the RCAF Air Navigation School (ANS) was first to make the station their home. They graduated airmen in "Wings Parades" every two months throughout this period. The Summerside base was one of only three air navigation schools in the British Commonwealth at the time.

Permanent married quarters were needed because of the expansion of the base, and in 1949 construction began. When complete, Slemon Park was a major re-vitalization of the base; it included an extension of the runways to the west. In the photo below, the expanded runway area can be seen clearly in the background. Four or five farm families had land to the west and north. It was clear that the RCAF base would remain in Summerside indefinitely. By 1951 the new No.1 Central Heating Plant was operational.

On the tarmac in winter, c.1947. Left to right: Digby, DC-3, Ventura, and Flying Boat aircraft.

In the 1950s a new era of navigator training started with students from NATO countries—including Italy, Norway, and Belgium—taking part in the first course and graduating in 1951. These wings parades were normally colourful and well attended both by the people of Summerside and by high-ranking military officials from NATO countries.

In 1953, the Air Navigation School was moved from Summerside and replaced by the No. 2 Maritime Operational Training Unit, which would remain until 1968. For the first few years, twelve Lancaster aircraft, converted for the training unit, flew in the skies over Summerside. Crews were trained for maritime patrol squadrons on the east and west coasts. In the late fifties, the training and patrol aircraft at Summerside began to reflect post-war technology. By 1956, the aging Lancasters had been replaced by the more sophisticated "Neptune" anti-submarine aircraft. Over the next couple of years, ten Neptune planes would be stationed in Summerside for training purposes. But the most exciting aircraft at Summerside was soon to arrive: the Argus. The official announcement regarding which Argus squadron would be stationed in Summerside was slow to come; however, it was clear by 1958 that their arrival was imminent. Construction and improvments costing at least eight million dollars were slated for the base, which was to build three new hangars to house six Argus aircraft. Other improvements included more central heating capacity, a fuel and armaments storage area, taxiways, and high intensity runway approach lighting.

When first purchased in 1955, all Neptune anti-submarine warfare aircraft were painted midnight blue.

Summerside expanded over the next few years by the addition of several hundred housing units at the north end of Granville Street—the Hillcrest Housing Development. The arrangement was to lease these units back to the Department of Defence.

This circa-1957 aerial photo shows the new school at extreme right (mid-photo), the new Prince County Hospital (above the school to the left), and part of the new nurses' residence (to the right of the hospital). The area above the hospital at upper right is the northward extension of the town of Summerside underway at this time. Beaver Street is at lower left.

For Summerside, the development created a major northward expansion that, for various reasons, continues to this day. The aerial photo on the opposite page shows the extent of northward development and the new Prince County Hospital and nurses' residence.

415 Maritime Patrol Squadron

In the spring of 1961, air force headquarters officially announced that Summerside would be part of the Maritime patrol fleet of Argus to be operated by a revived World War Two squadron—the "Swordfish." The six Argus aircraft arrived over the next few months and stayed in Summerside for twenty years, until the 415 Maritime Patrol Squadron was removed to Greenwood.

The era of the Argus at the Summerside Air Force Base was perhaps its finest. As the largest anti-submarine aircraft in the world, the Argus rattled windows as it passed overhead—and it was built in Canada. Summerside, along with Greenwood, Nova Scotia and Comox, British Columbia, was thus associated with world leadership in aviation.

Argus aircraft in flight with MPEU insignia visible.

The squadron arrived on base in early June of 1961. The first crew to arrive consisted of Flight Lieutenant Bill Misener, Flight Lieutenant Al Wolfenden, and sergeants George Doucette and Buzz Bezanson. Squadron Leader Bill Houser welcomed the the crew upon their arrival at RCAF Station Summerside. This squadron was given the task of providing anti-submarine and ship surveillance over the North Atlantic. "In 1961 Flight Lieutenant Misener and crew established a new airborne endurance record by completing a thirty-hour non-stop flight. This record was achieved on a normal Arctic surveillance patrol and covered over 5,200 miles." Over the course of its stay at Summerside the squadron took part in major exercises in the North Atlantic. It conducted anti-submarine warfare and fisheries patrols in Canadian territory, flew sovereignty patrols in the Arctic, and assisted search and rescue organizations at sea and on land in their search for lost ships and airplanes.

413 Transport and Rescue Squadron

As the 1960s came to a close, another major unit arrived at CFB Summerside—413 Transport and Rescue Squadron (a.k.a search and rescue squadron). As the prime search and rescue unit on Canada's East Coast, it oversaw 1,500,000 square miles. For two years the squadron flew the Albatross aircraft that they had used since 1960. In 1970 the Albatross were replaced by three Buffalo aircraft and three Labrador helicopters. Over the years the transport and rescue squadron continually lived up to its reputation as a team that would "go anywhere, anytime, at a moment's notice."

Three 413 Squadron helicopters in formation at Seacow Head lighthouse.

Spirit and Style at Mid-Century

With major construction and maintenance at the base and new housing developments, the social accommodations in Summerside began to evolve as well. Prior to the war there had been dances in the community for young people and adults, but the influx of military personnel flooding the dance halls created a larger demand. One such hall was the Maple Leaf Gardens, owned and operated by Reg Pope on the second storey of his building on Summer Street. People came and went by the busload to and from military sites such as Mt. Pleasant to attend dances. Concerns over the apparent relaxing of the community's morals were voiced, but in the end the changes had to be accepted as natural. Once the war was over, the Maple Leaf Gardens dance hall closed. Within a very short time Summerside's second movie theatre—The Regent—was established on the ground floor of the former dance hall. It was operated by the Pope family. Here, from the Peter Pope family collection, is a glimpse of the excitement on opening day of the theatre. With the war over, Summerside would swing into the 1950s.

Opening day at The Regent, c.1948. The line-up went around the corner onto Water Street.

RIGHT: **A sea of faces inside The Regent on opening day, 1947.**

The Imperial Dance Palace (also known as "The Diner" and "The Imperial Diner") opened its doors in St. Eleanors. Several groups from Prince Edward Island and the Maritimes played there. The Blue Notes, a local group that evolved into the Lowell Huestis Orchestra, played there in 1948, not long after it opened.

The Lowell Huestis Orchestra at the opening of the Summerside Stadium, 1955. Left to right are Lowell Huestis, Wilfred Arsenault, Ron Hutchison (drummer), Ed "Tooter" Baker, and Derwin Huestis.

Don Messer and the Islanders at The Imperial Dance Palace in St. Eleanors, c.1950. At the back are Charlie Chamberlain, Marg Osborne, and Warren MacRae, on drums. At the front are Jackie Doyle (piano), Don Messer (fiddle), Ray Simmons (clarinet), Harold MacRae (trumpet), and Duke Neilsen (trombone).

Marg and Charlie at the Tartan

Radio and early television helped make Don Messer's orchestra members Marg Osborne and Charlie Chamberlain famous. They are seen here at a casual venue, an after-hours party at Summerside's Tartan Restaurant in the early 1950s. Radio and TV became so powerful over the next twenty years that for a whole generation of Maritimers and later Canadians the mere sight of Marg and Charlie brought to mind the closing theme of Don Messer's show, "Till We Meet Again." The song is a haunting melody that ties the 1950s and 60s to the war years previous.

Smile the while
You kiss me sad adieu,
When the clouds roll by
I'll come to you,
Then the skies
Will seem more blue
Down in lovers lane
My dear...

The Maritimes' most famous orchestra of the era—Don Messer and the Islanders—drew hundreds from across the island. The magic of radio developed an audience for this non-traditional band with its blend of down east, traditional, and swing sounds—known as the "Don Messer style." To the delight of local dancers, Don Messer's Islanders took the place of the Blue Notes at the Imperial Dance Palace whenever they could.

Marg and Charlie at the Tartan Restaurant in the early 1950s.

ABOVE: **Bob Schurman, Jack MacAndrew, and Lowell Huestis broadcasting the action at the air show at RCAF Summerside (below), c.1952.**

The RCAF Summerside base remained an important part of the social life of the town. The George R. Pearkes, V.C. Branch, Royal Canadian Legion and the various clubs on the base facilitated this presence with great success through the 1950s and 60s. One of the highlights of the year was the annual air show, which threw open the gates of the base to the general public for demonstrations, stunts, and flypasts of various kinds. The new radio station in town, CJRW, broadcast the action to its listeners. Lowell Huestis and Bob Schurman were two of the chief on-air people, and Jack MacAndrew was in public relations with the air force.

According to several Summerside residents who lived through the post-war period, a complex series of changes resulted in radical changes to rural life and old values in the town. Folklorists call this period "the break." Maritime traditions were abandoned as the new technologies that were fast-tracked during the war started to find use in peacetime applications. Perhaps no image better conveys the confidence and

enthusiasm with which islanders took on the 1950s than the photograph at the bottom of this page, which was taken at the grand opening of the Island Equipment Company in Summerside around 1955.

Hudson Jeffery, Bedeque

Bedeque Bay farmer Hudson Jeffery cites the tractor and other farm machinery as primary examples of the kind of technologies moving in. Prior to the war, tractors were rare, but it seems almost everyone bought some form of farm machinery soon after. Hay balers and of course cars came along too. Those who could not afford tractors and cars continued to use horses. Jeffrey's first tractor, which cost him "a little horse" plus $1,400, was a 1950 Ferguson.

Man on a Massey Harris Challenger with spring tooth harrows behind, somewhere near Summerside, c.1937. First produced in 1936, the Challenger was Massey Harris' first row-crop tractor.

The showroom at the Island Equipment Company opening in Summerside, c.1955.

Summerside's commercial district would change in the next couple of decades, gradually becoming less concentrated in the Water Street area. The demands of the automobile would dictate that whole blocks where buildings were once crowded together be converted to parking lots. For fifty years the boundaries of the town had crept north, but in the fifties and sixties the town virtually burst northward.

Some of the town's leading gentlemen of the day appear in the following images. The first foursome includes, from left to right, Henry Noonan, the lawyer; Bill Roach, the barber; J.E. Dalton, the druggist; and Doc Wood, the veterinarian. Dalton's son George says the four friends were visiting the old Holland homestead at Tryon where cattled owned by Dalton were pastured. It was likely the late forties or early fifties when they posed so impressively in front of their circa-1940 two-door sedan.

A pose of a different kind occurs a few years later with a group of younger men at MacNeil Motors on Water Street East. From left to right are Harold Jones, office manager at MacNeil Motors; Keith Lapp, chairman for the "Y" Men's Radio Auction; J. Allie MacNeil, presenting the keys; and Ken Walker, president of the

The lawyer, the barber, the druggist, and the veterinarian.

"Y" Men's Club. It was 1957 and the car donated by MacNeil Motors to the annual "Y" Men's Radio Auction on CJRW was a 1954 Chevrolet.

J.E. Dalton, a druggist and owner of Gourlie's Drugstore, was one of the prominent citizens of the town. Druggists profited from the silver fox industry; besides carrying various pieces of equipment for handling and treating foxes, they sold animal health products such as flea powders, ear mite powders, and worm pills.

MacNeil Motors donates a 1954 Chevrolet as the grand prize in the annual "Y" Men's Radio Auction, 1957.

Of course, veterinarians benefited as well. Gourlie's was one among a number of drugstores in town. It operated at several locations in the old centre of town near the Central-Water Street intersection for about one hundred years, until 1965. The last of the independently owned and operated drugstores were MacDonald's, a smart combination of pharmacy and veterinary services, Foley's, Enman's, Boates', and Wedge's. The druggists who worked at these stores were also the last to mix their own drug compounds.

Chapter 5

Downtown Commerce

"She was a booming place for a while."

The surge of economic activity that followed the establishment of the RCAF Summerside Station carried forward into the 1950s and 60s. But eventually economic benefits brought to Summerside during this era would diminish, just as they had during the shipbuilding and silver fox eras. The fires and wars that also greatly affected the town caused one observer to remark, "it has been one thing after another that this town has rebounded from." To find evidence of the challenges faced by the community as it grew, we need look no further than the changing face of its commercial district.

Emerging trends in employment and transportation in the last half of the nineteenth century drew merchants from surrounding areas—Central Bedeque, Lower Bedeque, North Bedeque and St. Eleanors—into Summerside. Gradually the Acadian workers who moved into Summerside from the Evangeline region became entrepreneurs too, beginning with the Perry (Poirier) family in its operation of the Queen Hotel. Summerside was the major Prince County export and service centre—a seaport town catering to the farmers and fishers of the west half of Prince Edward Island.

The most active Summerside shippers of produce from 1855 to 1900 were J.C. Pope, R.C. MacLeod, Angus MacMillan, John Lefurgey, R.T. Holman, Capt. Joseph Read, and David Rogers. While they all left their mark on Summerside, it was Robert Tinson Holman who became known as the "merchant prince" of Summerside. He spearheaded a mercantile empire based on the department store model—"Everything from a nail to an automobile" or "Everything from a needle to an anchor" were two expressions describing Holman's diverse offerings by the 1920s.

R.T. Holman Limited

The name R. T. Holman is synonymous with Summerside, especially mercantile Summerside, in the latter half of the nineteenth and much of the twentieth century. R.T. Holman Ltd. was established in 1857 by Robert T. Holman. An import/export

Gaudet family in front of Holman's Garage, across from the main Holman department store on Water Street, c.1920.

company with wholesale and retail operations, it soon employed more workers than any other company on Prince Edward Island. Robert's older brother, James, is best remembered for the pioneering work he did in establishing the Island Park Hotel on Holman Island in the 1870s. He died suddenly in 1877; the hotel was closed and stood vacant until it was destroyed by fire in 1904.

Robert went on to become one of the most significant commercial figures in island history. He made a vital contribution to the economic development of Summerside and his family-operated merchandising enterprise was unequalled in the Maritimes. The construction of a splendid, three-storey brick store fronting Water Street crowned his mercantile efforts in 1893-94. Holman,

Drawing of the Holman complex in Summerside, 1915.

BELOW: Holman's staff in front of the Summerside store in June 1940. Third from the left in the front row is Adrian Casey, *not* a Holman employee. When asked jokingly as he passed by if he would like to get his picture taken, Casey surprised everyone by obliging! (See page 124 for a list of names.)

who likely knew the price and place of every item in his store, remained intensely involved in all things commercial until his death in 1906. His method was to keep a very close eye on all aspects of his business operation. His sons Harry T. and Le Roy (Roy) took over operation of the business in 1906.

In 1908 the new generation modernized advertising at Holman's, and an island institution was born—the Holman's mail order catalogue. R.T. Holman Limited cultivated the idea that theirs was the biggest "town store" in the Maritimes. The catalogue "was small and

RIGHT: Front page of one of the first volumes of the Holman catalogue, 1909.

A few departments of R.T. Holman Limited.

LEFT: The Soda Fountain with stools.

BELOW: The Christmas toys display.

The Drapery & Rug Department at Holmans, with Hoover cutouts on display in the foreground.

plain in appearance, but as the years passed expanded to a twice yearly (spring & summer and fall & winter) publication with two- and three-colour printing on the cover." Published until the 1930s, it made a valuable contribution to island society during its time.

On the inside, Holman's store was impressive, stretching for what seemed like miles upstairs and down, with a different department around every corner. This series of photos appears to date from the 1920s and was most likely taken to commemorate the store's seventieth birthday in 1927—the same year Canada celebrated its sixtieth birthday with a large parade on Dominion Day, July 1, 1927.

The Competition

While R.T. Holman Limited may have been the anchor of the service, manufacturing, and retail sector through the early twentieth century, it was not without competitors. Families tended to have a favourite store—some shopped exclusively at Brace McKay Company, while others spent their money only at Sinclair and Stewart. One previous long-time employee of Smallman's stated that customer loyalty was extremely important, so great pains were taken in serving customers and the time spent with them was usually considerable. It was a time when store clerks knew their customers by name. Credit for the competition's success can be attributed in part to R.T. Holman Limited, because in many cases both owners and staff of these other businesses received years of experience and training at Holman's before setting out on their own or being recruited by the competition.

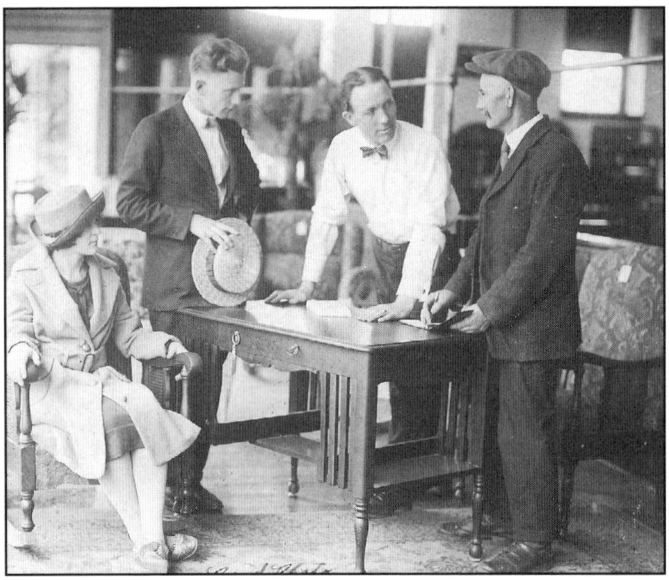

Newlyweds receive caring service at Holman's, c.1927.

The roots of Brace McKay Limited date back to the late 1880s, although under this name it carried on business from 1899 well into the twentieth century. The façade of the Brace McKay building had only recently been refurbished by M.F. Schurman Company Limited when, on February 6, 1958, one of Summerside's most spectacular fires hit. The building that burned had been built after the Campbell Hotel was torn down in 1903 and replaced by the Schurman Building on Water Street where it meets Summer. This section later became known as the MacArthur Block.

The Strong family operated a store on the corner of Central and Water streets until the mid-twentieth century. The Strongs had moved to this location in the 1870s from Bedeque after recognizing that Summerside would be a major new transportation centre for Prince Edward Island. When Strong's store went out of

BELOW: Brace McKay's first location, c.1890, on the ground floor of the Campbell Hotel, which was torn down in 1903 to allow easy access from Water Street to the new location of the post office on Summer Street (const. 1886).

BOTTOM: Brace McKay's second location —the MacArthur Block, 1914.

business, W.E. Smallman, one of the original partners of Sinclair and Stewart, bought the store and expanded his department store, which included grocery and hardware. The addition made room for a furniture and appliance store.

One of the town's major businesses, Sinclair and Stewart Company, has a history in the community that dates back to 1874. It operated on Water Street until the 1940s. For years it was *the* store for the discerning buyer—one source characterized it as the choice of the better-off among the townsfolk. Brace McKay Company, on the other hand, appears to have been the choice of the country folk, while Holman's seems to have done a good job of appealing to almost everybody. The Sinclair and Stewart Company

became known as Smallman's when W.E. Smallman took it over in 1947.

The commercial landscape of the town changed in the 1950s as retail business began to feel the influence of various national chains in such areas as personal needs and home furnishings. This had an impact on the streetscape as the signs for Simpson-Sears and CTC indicate.

The Brace McKay store is gone, the Royal Bank façade is changed, and national retailers Simpsons-Sears and CTC are on the north side of Water Street, c1960.

Scenes from Water Street

While it is important to note that the business district of Summerside spread beyond the bounds of Water Street, it is Water Street that many senior Summerside residents remember first and foremost when they recall the first half of the twentieth century.

The east end of Water Street more or less started at the corner of Harvard and Water Street East, where D. Alex MacDonald's Ford Lincoln dealership is located today. Some of the larger commercial outlets included Hall Manufacturing at the foot of King Street, and Bishop's Foundry on the opposite side of King. Morrison Brothers Beverages was also in the immediate area—a soda pop bottling plant whose upper floor came alive at night as one of the popular local dance halls.

In the 1930s M.F. Schurman was in the same location as it is today, although its 1940s and 50s expansions had yet to be

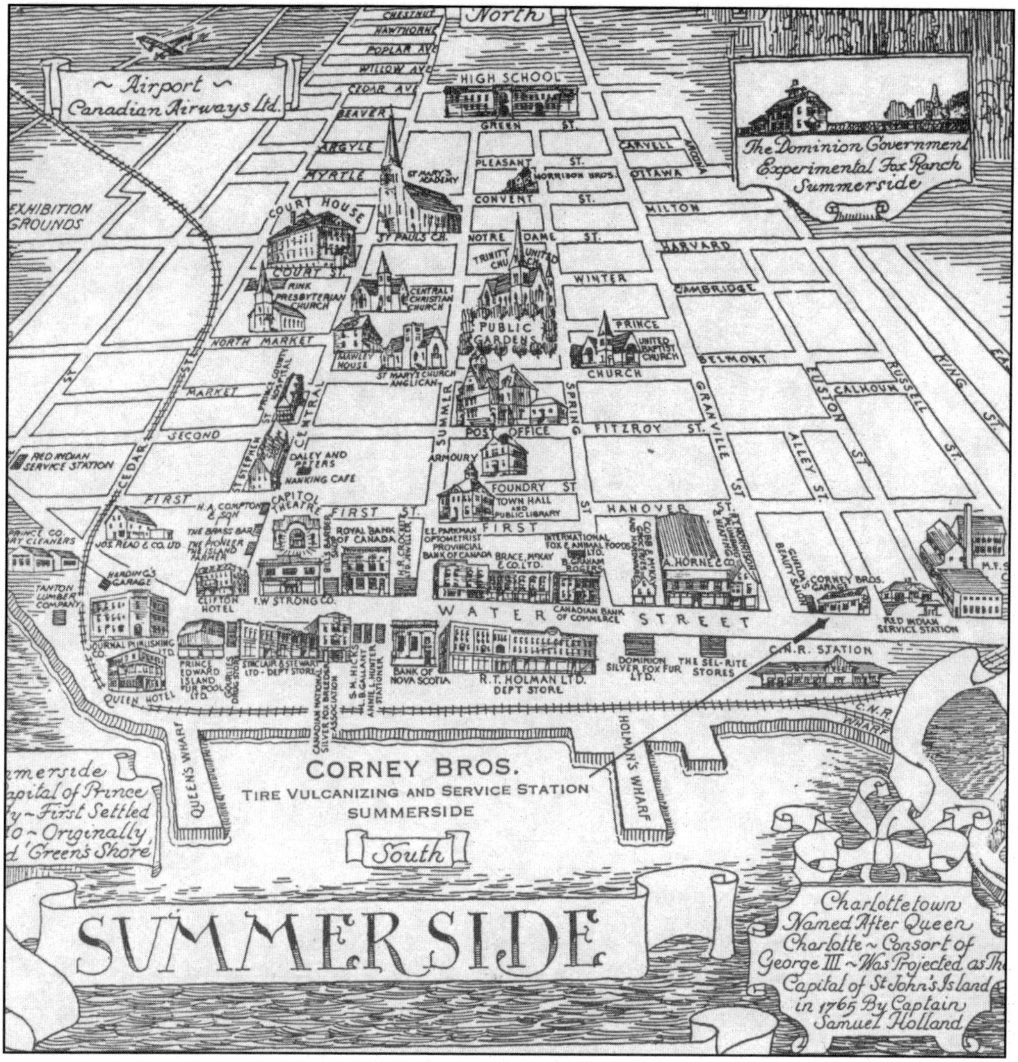

A 1934 map promoting Summerside. Note the business and civic landmarks. The airport was opened in 1934 and the Dominion Experimental Ranch reflected Summerside's leadership role in the still-vibrant silver fox industry.

started. Across Eustane Street from Schurman's was the Red Indian Service Station. And on the south side of Water Street was the harbour. While some in-filling of the harbour occurred over the years, most did not happen until the early 1970s.

The CNR Station re-located to a new building (now the Rotary Regional Library) in 1927. This was the third (and final) Summerside station and was more accessible to those travelling by car to catch the train. Where once Summerside had been the passenger destination for those leaving the province, now it was a stopover point where those travelling off island could catch a train to take them to the new departure point—Borden—to board the ferry.

ABOVE: **The east end of Water Street, viewed from the water, 1930s. Hall Manufacturing is among the cluster of buildings at the right of the photo.**

LEFT: **Hall Manufacturing Company.**

BELOW: **Red Indian Service Station, on Water Street at Eustane, c.1930s.**

Corney Brothers' garage, owned and operated by Art and Earl Corney, was located across the street from the train station. After serving in World War One, Art Corney joined his brother Earl at the bicycle shop on Water Street. Art always worked in the tire repair side, while Earl sold cars. The Leard brothers were among the various employees in the garage over the years.

Also on the north side of Water Street was Olympia Ice Cream, owned by Mr. Henry Gaudet (today the space is occupied

RIGHT: A lantern slide from Summerside's Capitol Theatre, 1920s, advertising Corney's tires.

BELOW: Irving Service Station and seawall viewed from the foot of King Street, c.1960. Earl McDonald's auto sales business shared street frontage with the station. Today a shopping mall and sprawling waterfront development exist on the water side of this service station location.

Cars for kings, and Kinkora

In small town politics, the Corney brothers played it smart. According to Frances (Corney) Lakhan of Summerside, on election day a car was provided for each party to use to drive their supporters to the polls. During the dry years of the 1930s, a "bottle of whiskey was given to each purchaser of a new car." Even layoffs had to be handled gingerly with small "p" politics in mind. One time, in the face of economic downturn, a man by the name of McIvor was let go, but he had to be hired back for fear of losing too many Chrysler sales from his home in Kinkora. Corney Brothers, being a Chrysler dealer, received the honour of looking after the Royal Tour Chrysler—remembered by so many islanders as the vehicle King George VI and Queen Elizabeth travelled in as they crossed the island in 1939.

The Royal Touring Chrysler from the 1939 Royal Tour pictured in front of Corney Brothers' garage with garage employees.

LEFT TO RIGHT: **Earl Corney, Arthur Corney, Russell Corney, Harold McIvor, Hazel Huestis, Roscoe Jeffrey, Albert Leard, Neil Marks, Charlie Peters, and Arthur Leard.**

by a dry cleaner). Kelly's Bakery was on the corner of Water and Granville streets, known among town elders as "Kelly's Corner." Crossing over to the south side, the "Fernwood Hotel" was located west of the railway station in a space occupied since the early 1990s by the Royal Bank. After the Fernwood Hotel was torn down, the CJRW building took its place. "A. Horne Chev-Olds" auto dealership was located across the street on the north side, between Granville and Spring Streets, in a space eventually occupied by Sobeys Food Mart (first of the large food chains to establish itself in Summerside) and toward the end of the twentieth century by Lo-Food.

Foley's Drugstore window, 1929. "You can't buy your blades in the bathroom," advises the mannequin.

The area on Water Street between Spring and Central was the financial section, where the larger retailers were also located. In the 1990s, the new Bank of Commerce building on the corner of Spring and Water streets was built on the same location as the old, but for a time the lot stood vacant. According to popular history, during the 1940s and 50s one of the town's better-known bootleggers used to hide his booze behind the high fence that surrounded the vacant lot. After being approached with an order on the street, he would disappear and return a few minutes later with a "teddy" (pint of liquor) or more.

Opposite the Bank of Commerce was the unofficial flagship of Summerside: R.T. Holman Limited, which started at the corner of Spring and Water streets, extending west along Water for a little less than two hundred feet. At ground level the town was dominated by the various storefronts and their grand displays. Through the richness of Sears Photography's collection, it is possible to experience some of downtown, perhaps as the townsfolk might have while out on a Sunday afternoon stroll in the 1920s or 30s.

Opposite Holman's on the north side was Frank MacKenzie's clothing store and to the west was a barber shop. Enman's Drug Store was west of MacKenzie's. Enman's, like most other drugstores, processed film and sold photo supplies, as evidenced seventy years later by the many postcards and prints with the Enman name on them.

Brace McKay Limited was located to the west of Enman's and included the MacArthur Block extending to the corner of Summer Street.

To the west of Holman's on the south side was the Bank of Nova Scotia. At the end of the twentieth century, a new Bank of Nova Scotia stands to the west of the old bank. Farther down the south side of Water Street facing Summer Street was Bell's Book Store, then Chan's Restaurant. To the west of Chan's was the Sheen and McInnis Shoe

ABOVE: Lantern slide from Summerside's Capitol Theatre 1930s, advertising MacKenzie's fashions for men. This store had a tradition of being a leader in men's fashions. Local advertising at the movies was very effective.

RIGHT: Pre-1927 photo of the Read Studio with its large north skylight and the Salvation Army in front, on the south side of Water Street near where the Bank of Nova Scotia is today.

Store. Both are visible in the Victory Arch photo on page 46, as is the Read studio building.

Around 1919 Mr. Harold R. Crockett and Mr. J. Edward Gallant posed in front of their new building, home to a jewellery store and a drugstore. While the cinder block façade has gone through several transformations, today the Crockett Jewellery store holds the rare distinction of being the only family retail store on Water Street to have survived the twentieth century at the same location.

At the opposite end of this block at Central Street was the F.W. Strong Limited building on Strong's corner, also known as Clifton House corner and Pope's corner.

This next street photo was taken from the west. Traffic could get congested, especially as people stocked up for winter. Prior to World War Two, roads were not plowed in winter and motor vehicles were put away until spring. In this photograph, an event of considerable importance might have been happening, possibly a fox breeders' event. The Canadian National Silver Fox Breeders Association headquarters was located nearby, on the south side of

Mr. Harold R. Crockett, jeweller, and Mr. J. Edward Gallant, druggist, pose in front of their new store on Water Street at Summer, 1919.

Water Street, and the vehicles, uniform in style, modern, and in the best of condition, were likely owned by successful fox ranchers.

Parking at a premium on Water Street, c.1938.

THE SURROUNDING FARMLAND SERVED BY THE TOWN

In 1900 the town continued as a fully functioning service centre for the surrounding countryside. The countryside was not far away as the early aerial photo of the intersection of Notre Dame and Duke streets (opposite page, right foreground) shows.

From 1888 onward the improved service that came with the introduction of the ice breaker *Stanley* extended fall shipments of produce through the port. When steamer service disappeared, the export tradition continued. There was less consolidation of land and agricultural operations; therefore, small, farm-based trucking was the norm. Over the years, Summerside would regularly export more potatoes than any other port in the world.

Summerside existed to serve the needs of the island agricultural community and beyond. Wise were the entrepreneurs and decision makers who followed R.T. Holman's pronouncement: Summerside owed its existence to one single factor more than to any other, that being the goodwill of a happy and productive agricultural county.

RIGHT: "Stooks" of grain, possibly in PEI's breadbasket—the Bedeque Bay area. This is one of the many "island scenes" that Don Sears loved to shoot in the late 1940s or 50s.

BELOW: Possibly the earliest aerial photo of Summerside, showing the west end from Notre Dame Street north to the water stand-pipe at the top of the photo, c.1931.

The following photos show the activities of the PEI Bag Company (founded 1935) and the workers at Hall Manufacturing Company (founded 1860s). Though they speak to different time periods, both companies, like many others in town, thrived upon meeting the needs of the agricultural community, and both became as specialized as possible. While the PEI Bag Company relied on burlap from far away India and Bangladesh to make its potato bags, the Hall Manufacturing Company depended upon steel and wood from closer to home and upon its relationship with Bishop's Foundry next door to make its farm machinery. Both companies succeeded in being inventive and focused on filling specific local needs first, with other markets soon following.

One of the countryside's demands was for locally designed and manufactured goods made from raw materials from near or far. Hall Manufacturing is gone but the Bishop's Foundry building, located on Water Street between King and Autumn (formerly East

Potato trucks lined up to unload to freighter at Railway Wharf, c.1950, when Water Street East was close to the water. Virtually all the harbour visible in this photo has been in-filled for the waterfront development.

Loading potatoes in Summerside

In the 1960s, the loading and shipping of potatoes was big business in Summerside, and farmers had begun to specialize in potato production by this time. Back in the late teens when one of the first farmers planted twenty acres of potatoes in the nearby Kinkora area, it was looked upon as a ludicrous experiment bound to bring financial ruin. But by the 1930s and 1940s, this kind of large-scale venture was catching on. George Key Jr. recalls that in the early days, long line-ups would form to the east of the Railway Wharf all the way past the Hall Manufacturing Company. There would be a team of horses and a sleighload of potatoes with a farmer on top waiting to unload at the warehouses or directly onto the boats. If the line-up lasted into the evening and the temperature dropped, the people of Summerside would come out with blankets for the potatoes and perhaps something warm for the farmer to drink.

An inside view of production at the PEI Bag Company in 1959, showing the giant press at right, and the sewing room, below.

Employees of Hall Manufacturing
TOP: l-r, back row: Matt Arsenault, Sandy MacArthur, Cecil Clough, Billie Cameron, Cliff Rankin; front row: Billie Gallant, Hubert Hall, Richie Rogerson. BOTTOM: Cecil Clough

Street), is still to be found in the city in the year 2002. The degree of self-sufficiency among the local manufacturers and tradespeople was impressive by any standard. Industrial employment and capital provided benefits locally. In the first half of the twentieth century there were shoe manufacturers, tailors, milliners, carriage makers, brick yards, and furniture makers along with the farm implement makers and foundries.

T. Johnston Company Plumbing & Heating storefront, 1915. Employees, l-r: Wilfred McElman, Cash Arsenault, Arthur Johnston, Bill Clark, Earl Brehaut, Frank Johnston, Thomas Johnston, Herman Callbeck, Jim Robertson, Rison Crossman, Roy Sullivan, Joe Shields, and Miss Harper (front and centre).

Chapter 6

Services in the County Capital

SUMMERSIDE became the county capital in the mid-1870s when the county courthouse moved from the original county capital of St. Eleanors to Summerside. It was incorporated as a town in 1877. Technological change, the constant threat of fire, and an unprecedented natural disaster all presented interesting challenges for the town of Summerside in the first seventy years of the twentieth century.

THE PRINCE COUNTY COURTHOUSE

Although it was a victim of the great fire of 1906, the Prince County Courthouse on Court Street, dating from 1874, was salvaged in 1908 by Peter Clark and D.R. Morrison. In 1938, it received a third floor in a major remodelling of the courthouse and jail. Led by Harold Schurman, M.F. Schurman Company Limited was awarded the $120,000 remodelling contract, a fact that made Schurman proud: besides being the leading symbol of Summerside's status as Prince County Capital, the courthouse was built by Schurman's maternal grandfather, Harold Beattie.

Prince County Courthouse, c.1939 not long after the re-modelling—note the curious child by the tree.

The Post Office—a gathering place

In the first half of the twentieth century, the Summerside Post Office was a place where folks gathered to share the latest news while they waited for mail fresh off the mail train or plane to be sorted. The railway station was another gathering place. Resident Herb Schurman had the privilege of working for both, starting at the post office in 1937 as office boy for $10 per week. Because Schurman had to wait for the mail train to arrive and be ready to work when it came in, his work hours were long and unpredictable. He started work at 6:00 A.M. in order to get all the mailbags that went east on the island and one "foreign" bag (for off-island mail) ready for the early morning train. Then, mail for points west to Tignish had to be sorted. Around 9:00 A.M. the Pig's Eye (the local name for the Summerside-to-Borden train) would come in.

In the early 1950s the federal government built a new post office at the corner of Central and Church streets. It opened in January of 1952, having been built by the M.F. Schurman Company of Summerside. In 1956 the old post office, dating from 1886, became the new town hall after fire destroyed the old one on Summer Street south of the Armoury. The clock tower, not part of the original structure, was added in 1914/1915 after citizens, led by the Board of Trade, suggested that the town needed an official timepiece.

TOP: Holman Gardens and Summerside Post Office, c.1902.

BOTTOM: Summer Street decked out with flags showing the Armoury, built in 1911, and the post office before the clock was added, c.1914.

A Flying Town

The Summerside Municipal Airport, though primitive by World War Two standards, was a major achievement for Summerside in the middle of the Depression. Located on a ridge overlooking Malpeque Bay to the north and Bedeque Bay to the south, and only three minutes from downtown, the airport consisted of a well-marked field with "standard size" runways 1,800 feet long and 500 feet wide.

The grand opening of the airport on August 13, 1934 was a momentous occasion attended by about three thousand people. Reg Pope helped convince ten fellow flyers who made up the aerial squadron of the Maritime Goodwill Tour to visit. The "gay galaxy of young mariners of the skies" promoted goodwill and flight and supported the town in their airport development. The idea was to exhibit the planes and take those who wished for a trip.

Blanche Kenny boarding the Lowneys' plane for a spin at the grand opening of the airport, August 13, 1934.

Wanda Wyatt was an early flier on the developing passenger service, flying to Moncton to catch the train to Montreal on April 9, 1935: "Dorothy and Mrs. Deblois sat ahead. Mother & I just behind & baggage in rear. There was not any sensation—we rose so easily and then all across the straits until we came over the Moncton Field—there was hardly a motion. Jones made a perfect landing on a soggy field. I doubt whether they make another trip until the fields are dried up."

An associate had to ride in another plane, an open one, and he ended up travelling with the mail into the train station for the trip to Montreal. This new mode of travel by which mail and passengers could reach the mainland was quickly embraced by Summerside folks.

In the mid to late 1930s, Canadian Airlines provided year-round service to most Maritime centres. In those days airports were far more basic than today's and the aircraft smaller and more versatile. In 1937 the runway at the three-year-old Summerside airport was expanded to accommodate an expected national airway system. Prior to 1937 the runway and airport consisted of not much more than an open field or two. A sea-plane base was also established at the Railway Wharf and served as an alternate trans-Atlantic port.

Canadian Airlines did serve the area for a few years, but by 1940 the airline made a request to the town council for improvements that would allow the landing of larger and faster aircraft. These improvements were required for Canadian Airlines to carry out their postal service contract between Summerside, Charlottetown, and Moncton. Within a year a legendary figure in Canadian aviation history, Carl Burke, a man who bought his first aircraft from Summerside's Reg Pope, had formed Maritime Central Airways (MCA). Summerside, which took to the air enthusiastically in the century of flight, would be an important link in the Maritime air network for the next several decades.

Maritime Central Airways (MCA) DC3 taking on passengers, c.1954.

Thanks largely to the work of aeronautical pioneer and local inventor Reg Pope, Summerside established itself early as a destination for flyers. Mr. Pope built his own planes in the room over his garage. (During World War Two the same room became the Maple Leaf Gardens Dance Hall.) Many Summerside residents owe their first flying experience to Pope and several early aerial images of the town and surrounding countryside can be traced back to those flights.

Little more than a decade after aircraft first flew over Prince Edward Island, Reg Pope was keenly interested in aircraft. He made news in 1931 in his Heath Parasol monoplane. The headlines bore witness to the Summerside amateur who flew to Moncton in his homemade plane. According to the *Moncton Times:*

> Mr. R. Pope, of Summerside, P.E.I., who built a small monoplane which is one of the first to be assembled in the Maritime Provinces, made a successful flight to the Moncton Airport in his sturdily-built craft on Monday. He made the trip from Prince Edward Island in good time. The machine has a wing span of 15 feet, is 20 feet in length and stands four feet high. The owner has only three hours solo flying time to his record in the air. He came here to get the machine tested out and pilot Burton Trevice accompanied him. The latter, after putting the small craft through the various tests, pronounced it as being one of the best ships he had ever flown.

Reg Pope's Heath Parasol aircraft, c.1930.

Delivering the goods

Municipal bodies as well as private enterprises were responsible for the delivery of community services. Mr. Urban "Sparky" Cameron was a long-time post office employee of a new generation—he worked at the post office after the change to door-to-door delivery. Over his twenty-six-year mail career, which stretched into the 1970s, he worked several routes, walking a total of 93,000 miles on the streets of Summerside. By the 1960s most of the other delivery men of Summerside —the iceman, the fishman, the milkman, the coalman, and the eggman, not to mention the blacksmiths and teamsters—were already or would soon become a thing of the past. The meatman and fishman carried on awhile longer, but only the postman continued through to century's end.

A few of the delivery men of Summerside.

BELOW: Milkman Albert Boswell delivered milk from his Hillhurst Farm around town in the 1920s and 30s.

ABOVE: Archie LeClair, described as a hard-working, strong, and capable coal man, in later years in the west end of town.

RIGHT: Unidentified sloven driver in front of the Dominion Express and McDonald Drug Company at the corner of Granville and Water streets, c.1910.

Snapshot of three Joes, identified by town historian Peter Pope as "Fat" Joe, Joe "Giblets" and Joe "Moose."

Working at the post office required a little creativity in keeping the names and identities of various townspeople straight. Among the large Roman Catholic Acadian population, for instance, lived a great many Josephs—often four or more bearing family names such as Arsenault, Gaudet, DesRoches, and Gallant. Summerside architectural historian Faye Pound has documented a number of names: Joe "the Island" Wedge worked on Holman Island (and later delivered coal around town); Joe "Holman" Gallant worked at Holman's; Joe "the Post" Richards transported the mail from the railway station to the post office; and many more, including Joe "Bunn" Gaudet, cafe and theatre owner.

Health Care

The lack of sanitary conditions in the first decades of the twentieth century meant that health care professionals had their work cut out for them. As late as 1900, the streets and squares were used as feeding ground in summer by horses, cattle, pigs, sheep, and geese. Many poor families needed these animals for

The downtown was densely occupied by buildings as this c.1931 enhanced aerial view of Central Street shows. The popular Market Hall (today a parking lot) is the large building in the foreground, while the Prince County Hospital (today CO-OP Basics) runs parallel to it behind and to the left. Beyond that is the nurses' residence in the old Summerside House (today Linkletter Inn & Convention Centre).

meat and dairy supplies and could not afford to travel to pastures outside of town. To compound matters, many citizens relied on public wells for their water supply.

In 1912, the new twenty-bed Prince County Hospital opened on Central Street; M.F. Schurman supplied the interior finishings for the new hospital. Maynard Schurman was a charter member of the hospital and a life-long supporter of the institution. In the tradition of community, one of the early fund-raising events in support of the Prince County Hospital was a dance at Fernwood House on Summer Street. The community tradition of rallying round the hospital cause was begun and continued through to the next expansion, which saw the second Prince County Hospital open on Beattie Street at the north edge of town in 1951.

Early medical doctors

Doctors Fuller, Price, Shrive, Jarvis, Bagnall, McKay, and McKelvie were some of Summerside's early doctors. With the establishment of the first hospital in 1912 the medical staff was headed by Dr. Alexander MacNeill and comprised of doctors Edwin Tanton, John F. MacNeill, A.A. MacLennan, John Jardine, E.E. Sinclair, along with F.W. Jardine from Kensington and Mark Delaney from Miscouche. Grace R. Beattie was the first superintendent of the school for nurses, located in the old Joseph Green inn known since the 1840s as Summerside House.

The original Prince County Hospital, at the corner of Central and Market streets, c.1915.

THE SUMMERSIDE FIRE AND POLICE DEPARTMENTS

With the many fires over the years the Summerside Fire Department could be excused if it felt a little beleaguered, especially when fire visited close to home. Citizens remembered with pride the great sacrifices made by their volunteer fire department. The youth of Summerside in this photo no doubt remembered imagining themselves as firefighters on the old and the new fire engines on a visit to the station in 1968.

Fire department engineer-caretaker Albert Leard shows the 1931 ladder truck to a kindergarten group in 1968.

The Summerside Police Department was equally attentive to the needs of children. In the photo on the next page, a crossing guard with the force provides safe crossing on Summer Street.

For most of the first half of the twentieth century, the Summerside Police consisted of only a handful of men. There had not been much change in numbers since the beginning of policing in the late 1800s. The fire that destroyed the town hall in 1955 also destroyed Police Headquarters. The department moved into cramped quarters in the old post office building, which was soon to become the new town hall. By 1963 the newly renovated garage section of the old town hall became police headquarters. The department had grown from a few men to the fourteen pictured below.

RIGHT: **A Summerside Police crossing guard at Parkside School on Summer Street.**

BOTTOM: **Members of the Summerside Police Force, 1963. FRONT ROW, l-r: Elmer Matheson, Stewart "Red" Berry, Harry MacKay, Donald Wannamaker (chief), Ben Schurman (special assistant), Keith Champion, and Siguard MacKinnon. BACK ROW: George Arsenault, Neil "Pop" Sharpe, Gordon Grady, Carl Newsom, Peter Mailman, Blair Buell and George Morrison.**

Streets, Horses, and Automobiles

One of the priorities of any town council is the maintenance of its streets. The pattern of streets in Summerside was determined by the manner in which the descendants of the original Green family divided up their farms over the years. Even today many of the "cross" streets running east to west in the older part of town south of Green Street do not line up in a straight line after intersecting each of the four main north-south streets.

Water Street—the first east-west route through town—came into being when the road to St. Eleanors was joined to the road leading into town from Wilmot. By 1878 the boundary on the west was Duke Street and the northern and eastern boundaries were defined by Green and Eustane streets respectively. The primary north-south street was Central Street, extending as it did all the way to the Western Road in Sherbrooke. The centre of town was where Central Street intersected with Water Street on its way to Queen Street and Queen's Wharf. Granville Street did not extend north to modern-day route # 2 until the Hillcrest Development was created in the 1960s. Sidewalks in the days before pavement were made of wooden planks, as this early Lorne Read photograph illustrates.

Planked sidewalks in front of Royal Bank and the MacArthur Block, on the north side of Water Street looking east, c.1908.

"The pavement council"

Earl Cannon, past president of the Chamber of Commerce, remembers very clearly the days before public services included paved streets in the town. The first pavement arrived in 1927 and the council responsible for its allocation became known as "the pavement council." Until the roads were paved, Mr. Cannon remembers that it was impossible to get a car through the town until mid-May. Summerside, like so many towns of the period, was famous for its muddy streets in certain seasons; since the late 1870s it had been better to take the train into town in wet times than risk getting bogged down in muddy ruts in the street.

The official photo of the "pavement council in chamber", c.1927. At back, l-r: J.E. Wyatt (Recorder and Town Judge); Mayor Winslow J. Lidstone; and Dr. T.E. Tanton (Health Officer). Seated at desks, l-r: Councillor J.F. Arnett (Assessors & Parks); Councillor M.F. Schurman (Property); Councillor John Grady (Finance); John S. Wright (Assistant Town Clerk); H.J. Massey (Town Clerk); Councillor J.Y. Phillips (Streets); Councillor J.J. McNally (Fire & Light); and Councillor Thomas Johnstone (Police).

Paving continued into the 1930s and 40s, a major accomplishment in public works during the Depression years. The official ceremony upon completion of the project included the civic elite, with the workers looking on.

The arrival of pavement was yet another signal that the automobile would surpass the horse in the struggle for the hearts of the island's travellers. Horses were in use everywhere, uptown and downtown, sometimes for pleasure travel, other times to transport people or goods. Mail was picked up from the train by horse and sloven. The Canadian National Express Company had a high wagon in the mid-1920s, but changed over to trucks during World War Two.

After the initial legislative battles to deny automobiles access to island roads, the horse made way more or less quietly, and those who preferred them, a little stubbornly. The automobile changed the environment and the daily existence of all islanders. The shift from the horse to the automobile may have been the biggest transportation revolution of the century, although it could be argued that the rise and fall of rail rivals it. Trains went from steam- to diesel-powered before disappearing altogether in the 1980s.

The Canadian National Express Company horse and high wagon, beside Holman's store, September 1924.

Horse racing was a popular pastime in early twentieth-century Summerside. The King Edward Stables, located close to the railway station, was named in 1936 in honour of the new king, Edward VIII. The hotel associated with the stables, originally called the Dominion Hotel, changed its name to the King Edward, but changed back again to the Dominion Hotel when King Edward abdicated the throne at the end of 1936. Livery

Horse and sulky in front of the King Edward Stables, c.1936.

BELOW: **Work horses on Water Street, c.1910 with transport sleds.**

stables and horse sheds were all around town. Farm families would take grist in to Robinson's Grist Mill across from present-day Irving Oil on Water Street East. According to one town resident, the men stopped at the Dominion Hotel for food while the women shopped. There was a livery stable at the other end of town near the Prince Edward Island Bag Company. Nearly all the shops had horse sheds; so too did churches and hotels.

In 1913 Ned Wyatt wrote to his wife: "The automobile is raising quite a commotion thing here in the County … I don't think they will be introduced for some little time." But only four years later, with railcar ferry service imminent, the roads were being opened to automobile traffic. One of the most vocal proponents of the automobile was fox rancher Frank Tuplin. Tuplin had his Pierce Arrow towed from the Railway Wharf to his house because automobile operation was banned entirely on Prince Edward Island from 1908 to 1913.

Tuplin's dream of an automobile-friendly island won out. Within a couple of decades, the glamour of the Fords, Chryslers, and Chevrolets could be seen everywhere. Because of the wealth

Millionaire fox rancher and promoter Frank Tuplin and friends in his Pierce Arrow, c.1912 in front of the Tuplin-Holman house on Beaver Street.

Cars and people at Cavendish shore, probably in the late 1920s.

that the silver fox industry brought, Summerside-area residents could perhaps afford an automobile sooner than other islanders.

By the 1930s and 1940s Summerside was as much a driving town as any, and Sunday afternoon outings in the car to places such as Cavendish were common. Not everyone could afford a car, so Summerside, compact and on level terrain, also remained a walking town, especially for young people. Corney Brothers' Garage, a former bicycle and carriage shop, sold automobiles, which by the 1920s were seen often, if not in the country, at least in the towns.

Car foreground, with horse and buggy in the background, on Central Street in 1923.

These images from the Frances (Corney) Lakhan Collection convey the glamour, popularity, and sex appeal of the automobile for the younger generation at the outset of the 1930s. The photos were labelled by Frances Lakhan's aunt, Blanche Kenny. LEFT: "The Boyfriends and I," May 24, 1930; BELOW: "The Old Knight and Fair Ladies," 1930; and "The Ford," May 1930.

LEFT: Dr. MacPhee's son and daughter in front of car, c.1930.

RIGHT: **Harold Gaudet and his flashy car on First Street, probably in the 1930s. The popular owner of the only movie theatre in town, Gaudet would park his fancy car in front of the Capitol Theatre and talk with patrons as they came and went.**

BELOW: **Looking east from the Journal building, c.1950.**

The Ice Storm of 1956

BELOW: View from the Lefurgey house: Trinity United Church spires are on the left and Epworth Hall is on the right.
BOTTOM: Notre Dame Street.

Three major disasters struck the town of Summerside, impacting delivery of town services in the first seventy years of the twentieth century. Two were by fire—one in 1906 and one in 1916. The third, perhaps the town's greatest natural disaster, was the ice storm of January 6, 1956. Major snowstorms come and go but the great ice storm left a unique but mostly temporary impression on the landscape and a long-lasting impact on the photographic history of the town. Because the town had been served by the electrical generation plant since the mid 1890s and had come to rely on electricity, the ice storm impacted its residents especially hard. In the countryside, rural electricity services had only become official government policy in 1955,

Ice storm damage: broken light pole at Water and St. Stephen streets, 1956. Residents tried in vain to walk to work the next day on ice-coated streets, but one after another power poles snapped in two, frightening residents and making travel impossible.

so it was not overly difficult for rural islanders to function without electricity for the several months it took to repair the damage. Summerside's power plant had served as far west as Mount Pleasant prior to the ice storm, but the losses were so great that only the immediate area of the town continued to be serviced afterward. Outlying areas were taken over by the Maritime Electric Company, which eventually purchased all local electrical power suppliers except that of Summerside. Even the worst sleet storm to hit Prince Edward Island could not dampen the pride of Summerside people in the electrical generating capabilities of their town.

Chapter 7

Summerside at Play and Sport

While the concept of leisure may not have been a familiar one for many Summerside residents, especially in the early part of the century when free time was at a minimum, even the most burdened found some time for small pleasures. As might be expected from a town founded on the shores of Bedeque Bay little more than two miles from Malpeque Bay on the north, water played a prominent role in Summerside recreation. In the first few decades of the century, whether on water or on land, sports and leisure activities were loosely organized and informal. Organized sport for youth arrived in the immediate post-World War Two period.

Summerside had always excelled in putting together hockey teams such as the renowned men's and ladies' Summerside Crystals teams, but after the war a new recreation department would bring up a whole new generation of athletic achievers in baseball too. Summerside's hometown spirit and pride were defended across the island and on the mainland by hockey and baseball teams alike. There were compelling performances in other sports too. Whatever the activity, having fun emerges as a common theme throughout Summerside's history.

An unidentified woman on a leisurely visit to the Railway Wharf, early 1900s.

At Play on the Water

Hunting, fishing, clamming, and spending time at the cottage on the shores of Bedeque and Malpeque bays were all popular water-related activities. Life at the Summerside waterfront often combined work and leisure activities, no doubt out of necessity. The working age of sail passed gradually. Residents confirm that during the 1930s and certainly into the 1940s the number and frequency of schooners in the harbour dropped off dramatically, but in the 1920s they were still quite common. Meanwhile, recreational sailing was always popular on the waters of Bedeque Bay. Ice on the bay from late December to late March provided food-gathering and recreational opportunities rolled into one.

The photo below shows a Summerside resident pulling a smelt shack down Summer Street to the harbour at mid-century, when hundreds of ice-fishing shacks would dot the bay. Not only was smelt a sought-after fish export and a cash source, it was also a way to feed the family. Out on the ice, the rituals of the smelt shack were raw and primitive. Ice-fishing was a way to pass the

Smelt shack going down Summer Street, c.1950s.

This photo was taken below the Queen Hotel and labelled "Ice Sports, Queen's Wharf, Jan 2, 1931." It features women ready to play hockey—inspired no doubt by the success of the Crystal Sisters ladies' champion hockey team.

BELOW: Pleasure boat between Holman's Wharf and Queen's Wharf, c.1930.

Daley's smelt shack, and seven people, c.1950.

long winter, enjoy the company of friends and the occasional snack and drink. The shack pictured at left was located behind Morrison's Beverages on Water Street East, close to where the "ice-road" from Bedeque met the Summerside shore. Until the mid-twentieth century, people crossed the ice because it was more direct than taking the roads.

This view of a pleasure boat, below, lends a sense of what the waterfront was like between the Railway Wharf and the Holman Wharf around 1930. Note the Holman water tower, no longer necessary after the late 1930s when the town improved the capacity of its water system by tapping into a deep well.

A Walking Town

BELOW: **Four Summerside women off to the New Annan races.**

Walking was one of the leading recreations of the early part of the century. Sunday afternoons would be spent visiting friends and neighbours up the street or across town. Dressed in their finest, young people would go downtown and walk around. Outside town, a popular summer event was the New Annan Races, held at a horse-racing oval located in a country field northeast of Summerside. In the late 1920s the races were held on Wednesday afternoons, as that was the traditional half-day when businesses closed. In later years businesses would close on Saturday afternoons. On Wednesday, August 25, 1927 diarist Wanda Wyatt notes briefly that she made a last-minute decision to go to the New Annan Races and attend a ball in Charlottetown afterwards.

One of the early taxi services in town, begun around 1930, was run by Tessie MacNeill, one of the legendary Crystal Sisters hockey team of the 1920s and 30s. She was still running Tessie's Taxi in the mid 1940s. One of the services that succeeded Tessie's Taxi was Flicker Taxi, which had a location on Spring Street.

ABOVE: **Young men in front of the Canadian National Express office downtown on Water Street, dressed up on a holiday or a Sunday afternoon, c.1923. Consisting of merchants and others, the group was part of what the locals called The Millionaires Club. They were, l-r in front: Carl Crockett, Eric MacKay, Reg Morrison, Leith Smith, Heartz Godkin, _____ Noseworthy; in back, Charlie Peters and Eddie "Eli" Arsenault.**

RIGHT: **Tessie MacNeill polishing her taxi in spring.**

Popular gathering spots

Two destinations were well-known by those who travelled on foot. One was the Leas' fox farm on Harvard Street next to the pond at the electric light plant, and the other was "the Hill" on Central Street, where people went to bask in the sun and have their pictures taken. The wall in front of the MacKelvie residence made a large impression on Summerside residents who loved to walk by it. The location remained popular throughout World War Two as visiting airmen arrived on the scene, escorting the local girls up the hill on sunny Sunday afternoons.

Leas' Merry Sunshine Fox Ranch on Harvard Street, a frequent walking destination, c.1916. Eunice, the daughter of local resident Joe Clough, is at right. BELOW: Young men at "the wall," 1927.

View from "the Hill" on Central Street looking south in front of MacKelvie's wall at left, in the 1920s.

Theatre: Live performance and Movies

A moving picture theatre first arrived in Summerside in 1911. Happyland Theatre was first located in Market Hall on Central Street, at the corner of Central and First streets not far from where owner Joe "Bunn" Gaudet lived. His brother Henry Gaudet and Roy Silliphant were also owners. The Happyland Theatre created magical memories of the silent movie era—the piano player accompanying the action, creating his or her own music to fit the drama on the screen.

Market Hall was established in 1885 on Central Street just north of where the Guardian newspaper office is today. From 1911 until 1921 Happyland Theatre for "moving pictures and illustrated songs" was located in a large room with a stage and low-backed benches on the second floor. The Happyland sign is barely visible in this photo.

Souvenir tray from the Happyland.

In 1922 or thereabouts, Mr. Gaudet replaced the Happyland Theatre with the new Capitol Theatre—an enterprise that was to last until the end of the twentieth century and see four generations of the Gaudet-Perry family manage it. Talking pictures arrived in 1929.

ABOVE: A line-up for bicycles at Holman's stretched as far as the Capitol Theatre, c.1930. On crowd control are Joe "Bunn" Gaudet with megaphone, his son Harold in white shirt, and theatre projectionist Edmund Doucette next to the pole at right.

ABOVE: The Capitol Theatre exterior in the early 1940s, showing *Edison the Man* starring Spencer Tracey. The Tea Room later became a separate entrance to the downstairs bowling alley. Harold Gaudet, son of original owner-operator Joe "Bunn," was responsible for the renovation.

LEFT: Moving pictures—the *Rio Rita* is advertised on a local auto, with artwork by long-time Capitol Theatre employee Cyrus Arsenault.

BELOW: **The Capitol Theatre screen after re-modelling in the late 1930s, and the theatre's new concession stand.**

The Capitol Theatre was an entertainment complex that featured bowling alleys in the basement and the Capitol Tea Rooms in an adjoining building to the south. There was a pool room in back of the restaurant and a dance hall on the second floor. In 1937 a major renovation of the Capitol Theatre, including a re-design of the interior by Harold Schurman of M.F.

Schurman Company, was undertaken. The results, according to *The Island Farmer*, were "highly creditable to his [Schurman's] artistic ability and splendid workmanship as well as to the firm to which he belongs and the Capitol Theatre and management" (MacFarlane).

Downstairs at the Capitol Bowling Alleys.

Live theatre was no stranger to movie houses like the Capitol and the Happyland, as both could modify their screens into a broad performance stage for local and travelling theatrical events. As in the nineteenth century, theatre troupes of varying origins toured the community halls and theatres of the island, a tradition that dates back to the Chautaqua travelling shows popular in the 1920s and 30s.

Chautaqua came to Summerside in September 1927, and was attended by Wanda Wyatt and friends. From left to right: Amy, Linkletter, shepherdess; Ruth McPhail, bridegroom; Dorothy Brennan, bride; Wanda Wyatt, Grecian; Dorothy Wyatt, page; Lenore Chapman, mother-in-law; Dorothy McSweeney, Armenian; "Nayphe," Julius Caesar in front.

From the late 1940s to the early 1960s, churches and service clubs such as the Lions Club would sponsor and develop minstrel shows, a common practice in many communities in various parts of North America since the late 1800s. Herb Schurman was one of a large number of frequent performers in these shows, starting in the late 1940s for the United Church. Because roads were better by this time it was practical to tour by automobile to the west and east of the island. But first the minstrels played to packed houses in Summerside for as many as three nights running.

The Minstrel Show, sponsored by the Summerside Lions Club and held at the local school gymnasium, c.1960.

Just how much times can change in favour of better understanding among people is evidenced by the image above. A mere forty years ago a minstrel show scene like this one provoked little comment, whereas today it is virtually impossible to comprehend. The skits and songs performed often included a local story adapted to a well-known tune borrowed from the minstrel shows of the American south. The performers remember the shows as a well-meaning attempt at entertainment, a great deal of fun, and highly successful. But putting on black faces and using African-Canadian (and American) culture for humour was finally seen for what it was—a form of racial discrimination. This shift was aided in part by the advent of television, which brought the realities of racism and the struggles of the civil rights movement from the streets into the living rooms of North America.

Although the minstrel show format was dropped, the tradition of community theatre lived on and the voices that loved the old songs from the Chautaqua days and Sunday evenings around the organ would keep on singing. Meanwhile radio and TV left the distinct impression that the world was swiftly shrinking.

Getting the Message Out—Early Radio

The world's great divides of distance and space began to shrink noticeably with the arrival of AM radio in the 1920s. Like millions across North America, Summerside residents were enthralled by the magic of the new technology from the arrival of AM radio in the 1920s through to the 1950s when television grabbed the spotlight. Radio arrived on the wings of Summerside's mercantile sector. What had begun as a hobby of amateur radio enthusiasts R.T. Holman Limited turned into Summerside's first AM broadcasting station. Operating from the third floor of the brick store by 1927, Holman's adopted the call letters "CHGS," which stood for: *Call Holman's Guaranteed Satisfaction*. The Holman dynasty immediately saw the advertising power of the new medium. By late twentieth-century standards the station was minuscule, but for its time it offered a fairly complete service. It had two aerial broadcast towers atop the department store and the power output was only twenty five watts, which allowed it to reach a radius of thirty miles. By comparison, Mr. Wylie Barrett's amateur radio output in the 1990s is 1000 watts. Mr. Barrett, a native of North St. Eleanors, was one of the first people to work at CHGS. He recalls that the radio control rooms were very sparse, located as they were on the second floor above the hardware department and next to a freight elevator. The studio and control room were side by side with one door between them; the wall, however, was solid brick. The power was supplied by a motorized generator. Programming consisted of only a few hours daily and church service broadcasts on Sunday. In addition to live

CHGS Radio letterhead, 1930s.

Wylie Barrett singing over CHGS in the 1930s.

programming such as those by the Red Cross and entertainment from local orchestras like Gaudet's Oldtimers, there were programs of recorded music. The station continued until 1947. After a brief respite, the new, locally owned commercial station CJRW began operating.

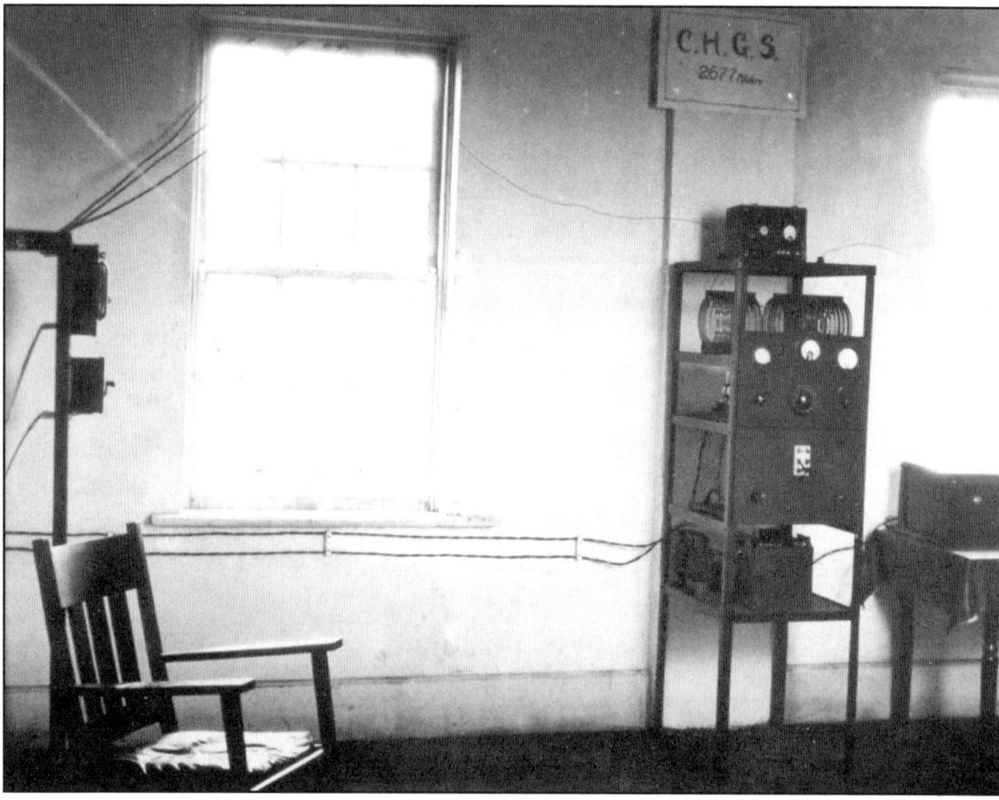

The sparse interior of CHGS, Summerside's first radio station, when newly opened in 1927.

Merchants were tuned in to the new technology in other ways. Former Chamber of Commerce manager and St. Eleanors native Earl Cannon remembers that the radio at his uncle's store attracted customers. "Amos and Andy" was the first popular comedy show and a soap company sponsored the Lux Radio Theatre on Thursday nights. Similar shows were sponsored by soap companies on TV as well, which is why they are known today as "soaps." Local shows featuring amateur talent were extremely popular on the new station.

Parades and the birth of the Summerside Lobster Carnival

In the 1950s, recreation, entertainment, local commercial promotion, and tourism were combined at mid-summer to create the Summerside Lobster Carnival. A community-sponsored event, it was the first of its kind on Prince Edward Island. The week-long event was organized for the middle of July and included a midway at the Summerside Raceway, exhibits of local crafts and baked goods, a "Miss Summerside Lobster Carnival Pageant," and a grand parade.

Whether military or civilian, parades in Summerside were always popular. In the 1950s one of the most unforgettable floats was the Planters Float. Who could forget it and the thousands of peanuts that covered it? This photo is from the 1950s (possibly as late as 1956), when the inaugural Summerside Lobster Carnival was held.

Community businesses supporting the Lobster Carnival were listed in the centre fold of the program, creating an invaluable record of the community spirit of the time. One of the trademarks of community festivals from the 1950s until the 1970s was the beauty pageant. Summerside's Carol MacKinnon went on from Prince Edward Island to win the Miss Canada title in 1968.

The Planters Peanuts float on Water Street in the 1950s.

Mayor Wedge was a popular leader from the Acadian community, which at mid-century comprised about half of the population of Summerside. In the first few decades of the twentieth century, a steady influx of Acadians largely from the rural Evangeline area just west of Summerside gave the town a distinctly Acadian flavour, as reflected in long-established island names like Arsenault, DesRoches, Doucette, Gaudet, Gallant, and Wedge. The Acadians maintained their rural roots by attending events such as the Agricultural Exhibition, held at Egmont Bay since 1903.

The grand opening of the Summerside Raceway on July 1, 1953, with Prime Minister Louis St. Laurent and Summerside Mayor Henry Wedge (at the podium).

Summerside, The Sports Town

There were three huge sports stories in the first seventy years of the century: the Crystal Sisters hockey team, Charlie Cahill's unique hockey exploits, and Alfred Groom's pole vaulting at the national and international levels in the early 1960s. Countless other stories unfolded as the town developed into an important sporting centre. *Journal Pioneer* writer and island sports icon John "The Realm" McNeill helped to bring the most important events and figures of the community to life.

John "The Realm" McNeill

BELOW: **The Crystal Sisters of Summerside—1926 PEI Hockey Champions.**
BACK, **l-r: Ella Gay, Anne Green, Helen Leard, Dot Weeks, Claire Mountain, Pat MacLellan.**
FRONT. **l-r: Tessie McNeill, Nora Green, Cornelia White, Fosta MacCulla, Miriam Leard.**

The Crystal Sisters were undefeated Maritime Champions from 1926 to 1935 and Eastern Canadian Champions from 1935 to 1937; they lost only one hockey game in eleven years, making them the most successful Prince Edward Island team ever.

Charlie Cahill, the first Prince Edward Islander to play in the National Hockey League, c.1927.

Charlie Cahill made the leap to the National Hockey League in 1925, going from the Summerside Crystals, contenders for the Maritime crown, to the NHL's Boston Bruins. The Summerside Rink, built in 1954, was renamed Cahill Stadium in his memory.

Alfred Groom held the Canadian pole vaulting championship for four and a half years and twice set a new Canadian record, the last time at 14 feet 3 3/4 inches in 1962. He won the Canadian Olympic

Pole vaulter Alfred Groom.

trails of 1960 at Saskatoon and the British Empire and Commonwealth Games trials twice. He represented Canada at the Empire Games of 1962 in Perth, Australia.

Looking back over the years at some of the big championships, it is clear that Summerside was and is both a baseball and a hockey town. In 1913-14 the Summerside Crystals hockey team won the Maritime championships—the first time ever for a Summerside team. In 1900 and 1908 they came close, winning the island championship. Two wars later the team had a new name—Summerside Aces.

The mid-1960s saw the beginnings of the Prince Edward Island Sports Hall of Fame in Summerside. People like James Hogan, the town's first director of physical fitness, and Charlie Hogan, a coach who succeeded against overwhelming odds, have been recognized in the Prince Edward Island Sports Hall of Fame for their accomplishments.

Robert (Bob) Schurman and Lowell Huestis of CJRW broadcasting a hockey game back home to the Summerside fans from the Charlottetown Forum, c.1952.

After World War Two, CJRW became synonymous with sports broadcasting and a leader in that department in the Maritime Provinces. In those days the broadcast and colourful commentary were impromptu in many ways—notice in the photo at left that the commentators are without notes or primers. Reporters Robert "Bob" Schurman and Lowell Huestis were broadcasting a game at the forum in Charlottetown back to the loyal fans in Summerside. The Summerside-Charlottetown rivalry, particularly in hockey, was one of the strongest ever seen in Maritime sport. Spectators would board special trains from either end of the island to catch the major games of the 1930s. Music and the singing of team booster songs punctuated these train trips—less so on the way home if the team lost.

The Summerside Paperweights, island champions of 1948-49.
BACK, l-r: : Garland Harris, Stan Gay, David Silliphant, Ron Mullins, Donnie Gay, Garth Harris. FRONT: Don Ross, Carl Delaney, Lester DesRoches, Greg Deighan, and Bobby Watson. Coach Bill Fridgen stands at the back.

Despite increased organization in the post-war years, backyard hockey continued on outdoor rinks such as the Kinsmen Rink on Granville and Carvell—the setting for hours of outdoor fun.

In baseball, as in other sports in the Maritimes, supremacy was a measure of success. From 1947 to 1951 the Summerside

"Lippy's Mites," 1952 at the Kinsmen Outdoor Rink. FRONT, l-r: Richard Gallant, Wayne Gallant, Dewey Trainor, Wayne Trainor, and Allan Gaudet. BACK: unidentified. Ernest "Lippy" Gaudet was a renowned player from the Summerside Crystals hockey team.

All-Stars, later the Curran and Briggs team, went to the Maritime baseball finals, winning it three years running—1948-50. The final win was off the bat of Summerside's Joe Dimaggio, Les Gaudet, a leader on and off the field, who went to bat with the bases loaded. No ordinary grand slam homer resulted when the ball came off his bat and flew out of the park, bouncing between two nearby houses and rolling down a hill, where it hit a rock and bounced into the back of a half-ton truck passing by on a lower road. In the early 1990s sports writer John "The Realm" McNeill wrote about Gaudet's homer, noting that "The hit is still in the memory of many over four decades later." McNeill was the *Summerside Journal's* first Sports columnist, spending well over fifty years at the typewriter from 1945 onward.

BELOW: Les Gaudet swinging the bat. "The grand-slam hero of 1950" became known as Summerside's Joe Dimaggio.

Outside of hockey and baseball there was a host of sporting activity ranging from golf (a course was established in 1927), to curling. Summerside had the first ladies curling club on Prince

1948 Maritime Baseball Champions (photo by Heckbert). FRONT ROW, l-r: L. Gaudet, R. Phaneuf, J. Grady, G. Williams, S. Bernard, F. Oatway, "Doc" McMurdo, H. Landry, Bill Allen (Capt). MIDDLE: H.Gallant, P. Mickus, G. Bernard, Pony Daley, B. Schurman, D. Carson, C. Powell. BACK ROW: J. McNeill, H.B. Schurman, C.Hogan. Mascot in front – D. LeFurgey.

Marguerite (Ben Alfie Arsenault) Raynor and Irene Godkin enjoyed hunting the wetlands of the Summerside isthmus as much as their husbands, who taught them the skills. In this photo the women take aim from the Raynor farm, north of Summerside, in 1961.

Edward Island and it hosted the first ladies bonspiel on the island, which was held at the Summerside Curling Club on March 16, 1951. The harbour was popular for swimming and yachting. The "fashionable" teenagers belonged to a tennis club in the 1920s. Bowling at the Capital Bowling Lanes was a popular sport with much city recreational league activity. And Summerside was no stranger to the "sport of kings," with a fine horse-racing track in the west end of the town.

Out on the bay, motor boating, sailing and, in winter, ice-boating and snowshoeing were all popular. Existing on an important north-south waterfowl flyway, the bays on both sides of Summerside provided ample hunting grounds for hunters. Fly fishing on the Dunk River—a destination for those looking for a day or two escape from the big city—was extremely popular in the early years of the twentieth century. Emptying into Bedeque Bay a few miles east of Summerside, the Dunk remained an angler's paradise through most of the twentieth century. The

BELOW: **Three hunters with many geese on the mud flats.**

Canadian Trade Review said of it in 1900: "But certain it is that this place is full of trout, which, coming in from the sea in springtime, retain throughout the season their rich saline quality. Great facilities abound for camping and many citizens and visitors take advantage of them for outings."

The Summerside Raceway and the hockey arenas near it were in the west end of town. In the photo at the bottom of the page from 1952, times were relatively good when construction of the raceway grandstand was underway. The seaward guardian of all the town—the Indian Head Lighthouse—is a faint shadow off in the distance. The inset photo is the home of Bowness Photography Studio illustrator Alphie Gallant, taken when times were tough. But baby brother Gerard, not yet born at the time of the photo, says theirs was a happy family—the children played, interrupted only by the fascination of the camera.

RIGHT: The home of Bowness Photography Studio illustrator Alphie Gallant, c.1933.

BELOW: Construction of the raceway grandstand, 1952.

As the century passed, motor boating gained in popularity and owning one became a sign of status in the community. In the photo below, well-known Acadian entrepreneur Harold Gaudet takes a number of friends out for a spin on Bedeque Bay in his famous mahogany motor boat. Once turned around, he would without a doubt pass the historic Indian Head Lighthouse and head out across the Northumberland Strait. Since the 1880s, the Indian Head Lighthouse has marked the entrance to Summerside. It continues to symobolize that which makes Summerside and the bay an attractive place to live, do business, and play.

RIGHT: The Indian Head Lighthouse.

BELOW: Harold Gaudet and friends in his motor boat on Bedeque Bay, probably in the early 1950s.

Image Sources

The gathering of images and information for this book was facilitated by many individuals, including: Windsor Corney; Lloyd Lockerby; Errol Laughlin; Marilyn Linkletter; Elizabeth (Strong) Reagh; Paul H. Schurman; Mike Schurman; Julie Simmons; Jim Peters; Claudia Rogers; Randy Ross; the late Guy Rodd; John "The Realm" McNeill.

The following list indicates the names of collectors who made images available for this publication.

Arsenault, Marguerite "Ben Alfie," Page 120(upper); Barrett, Wylie, Page 111(lower); Cameron, Urban "Sparky," Page 70(middle); Clark, Howard, Page 106(lower); Confederation Centre Art Gallery and Museum, Page xii; Daley, Gerald, Pages 59, 68, 69, 103(upper right), 105(middle), 113(upper); Dalton, George Pages xviii, 42, 58, 71(upper), 74(upper), 99(upper), 119(upper); Gallant, Gerard and Florence (Campbell) Gallant (includes collections of Alphee Gallant and Mary (O'Connor) Campbell), Pages 2, 7 (upper), 46(upper), 74(lower), 76, 106(upper), 107(upper), 107(lower), 108(upper), 114; George R. Pearkes V. C. Branch, Royal Canadian Legion, Huestis, Lowell, Pages 41, 43, 44, 45(upper), 48, 49, 56, 111(upper), 117; Huestis, Sonny, Pages 12, 98(upper); International Fox Museum and Hall of Fame, Pages xiii (lower), 13 (upper), 14, 77(lower), 87(lower); Johnston Plumbing and Heating, Page 80; Lakhan, Frances (Corney), Pages 72, 83, 93, 94(upper), 97(all four), 103(upper left), 104 (upper, and lower left); MacNaught History Centre and Archives Collection, Pages xiii (upper), 63(upper); McNeill, Tanton, Page 47(upper); Newsom, Carl, Page 90(lower—photo by Heckbert); PEI Bag Company Collection, Page 79(all photos by Heckbert); PEI Sports Hall of Fame, Page 116; Perry, Emery, Pages 107(middle), 108(lower), 109(upper), 121; Pope, Peter, Pages xvi, xvii, 21 (lower), 24(upper), 50, 53, 61, 85, 86(middle), 87(upper); Prince Edward Island Regiment Museum, Pages 39, 40(upper); Public Archives and Records Office(PARO) (including images from the Jack Turner fonds; the Colonel Hunt fonds; and the Jean Ronahan Collection, the Holman collection), Pages xv, 27(Turner), 28(Turner), 29(Turner), 30(Turner), 55(Ronahan), 82(upper—

Holman), 101(Colonel Hunt fonds); Read, George, Page ix; Savidant, Mildred, Page 80(upper and middle); Schurman, Herb, Pages 6, 92, 104(middle), 105(upper), 110; Sears Photography (including images by Lorne H. Read), Pages vii, viii, ix, x, xv(upper), 4, 5, 11, 16(upper),17, 21(upper), 22, 23(lower), 26, 27, 32, 33, 34, 35(upper), 36, 37, 38, 40 (lower), 52, 57, 62&63(lower), 64(upper), 70(upper and lower), 71(lower), 73, 77(upper), 78, 89, 90(upper), 96(upper and lower), 99(lower), 102, 103(lower), 105(lower), 107(upper), 112, 113(lower), 115, 120(lower); Summerside and Area Historical Society (includes John Hopkirk Collection and images from "Down at the Shore"), Pages xv(lower), 1, 3, 7(lower), 8, 13(lower), 16(lower), 18, 23 (upper), 24(lower), 25, 27, 35(lower), 45(lower), 46(lower), 51, 62(upper), 64(lower), 65, 66, 67, 75, 81, 82(lower), 84, 86(lower), 88, 91, 94(lower), 95, 98(lower), 100(photo by Heckbert); Summerside Recreation Department, Pages 118(both), 119(lower, photo by Heckbert); Thompson, Wilfred, Page 86(upper); Wyatt, Wanda (Wyatt Heritage Properties), Pages xiv, 109(lower).

The following list accompanies the photo on pages 62 and 63.

R.T HOLMAN STAFF
June, 1940
First Row: Robert L. Shaw, Louis Ranahan, Adrian Casey, D. Eric Woodside, Norman Hogg, Benj Gallant, J.LeRoy Holman, Robt. L. Mollison, Wm. A. Currie
Second Row: J.Borden Connell, Irene Silliphant, Gerald Major, George Spears, Errol Laughlin, Earle Boates, Leo DesRoches, Doris LeBlanc, Muriel Carver, Rita Ranahan, Gerald Smith, Davis Murray, Claude Harkness, James MacArthur, Ceyo Gaudet, Alden Leard, John Owen, Stanley Dawson, Robert Ferguson, W.W. Baker, Helen Doyle, Anne Linkletter, Claude Hopgood
Third Row: Joseph McLellan, Gordon Toombs, Cleve Whalen, William G. Ellis, Reta Gamble, Irene Peters, Georgie Huestis, Florence McInnis, Peggy MacCallum, Hazel MacCardle, Florena Linkletter, Hazel Clow, Albina Blanchard, Georgie Schurman, Margaret MacEwen, Thyra Bingham, Emmie Duncan, Irene Gallant, Albon Gillis, George Richards, George P. Walker, John Hogg

Fourth Row: John Green, Chas. Mountain, J.C. Mountain, Mildred Arthur, Wanda Bradshaw, Dorothy McDougall, Helen Harkness, Peggy MacDougall, Helen Clark, Ella Gay, Ferne Dystant, Jean Walker, Marion Woodside, Lilian Hogg, Freda Dingwell, Margaret Sinclair, Marion Connell, Eileen Richard, Victor Chaisson, Max Robertson, Ben R. Sharpe, Wallace Bradshaw, Arthur MacDowell, Hilbert Johnston, Joseph Cheverie
Fifth Row: Emmett Ranahan, Henry Bernard, Arthur Perry, Reg Hawkins, Hillard Arthur, Niel Durant, Anthol McNevin, Gerald Matthews, Wilfred Woodside, Wylie Barrett, Charles McIvor, Roland Murray, John Corbett, James Warren, Ray Perry, Fred Gallant, Lloyd Perry, Frank Gallant, Rennie Arsenault, Theodore Richards, Ray Bernard, Jack Arsenault, Alderic Richards, Issac Arsenault, Phillip Gallant, Lawrence Clow, Clarence Doyle, Frank Martin

Members of staff not in picture: Harry T. Holman, Pres, Harry T. Holman Jr. , Donald Baker, Harry Arsenault, James Connell, Earl Perry, Josephine Murphy, Hal Walsh

BIBLIOGRAPHY

The sources consulted in the research for this book include published and unpublished materials as well as formal and informal interviews with a number of individuals.
The main influences among the sources are:

Forester, Joseph E. and Anne D. *Silver Fox Odyssey, History of the Canadian Silver Fox Industry*. Canadian Silver Fox Breeders Association/PEI Dept. of Agriculture, 1982.

Gunn, Paul. *The Silver Fox Industry on Prince Edward Island*, B.A. thesis submitted to the Department of History, Mount Allison University, 1973.

Kessler, Deirdre. *A Century on Spring Street.* Indigo Press: Charlottetown, PEI, 1999.

Leard, George A. *Summerside Saints and Sinners: A History of Trinity United Church.* Published by the author: Summerside, PEI, 1958.

MacFarlane, Margaret. "History of M.F. Schurman Co. Ltd." Published by M.F. Schurman Company Ltd.: Summerside, PEI, 1995.

MacLeod, Ada. "The History of Summerside," *Summerside Journal,* 1923.

Morrison, J. Clinton Jr. *Hell Upon Earth: A Personal Account of Prince Edward Island Soldiers in the Great War, 1914-1918.* Published by the author: Summerside, PEI, 1995.

National Department of Defence, Government of Canada. *Forty Years 1941–1981: A History of the Base at Summerside*, 1982.

Pound, Faye. "Heritage Walking Tour." Published by the City of Summerside: Summerside, PEI, 2000.

Rankin, Robert Allan. *Down at the Shore: A History of Summerside, Prince Edward Island* (1752-1945). Prince Edward Island Heritage Foundation: Summerside, PEI, 1980.